# Power and Empowerment

## Neil Thompson

**TiP** Theory into Practice

Series Editor Neil Thompson

**Russell House Publishing**

First published in 2007 by:
Russell House Publishing Ltd.
4 St. George's House
Uplyme Road
Lyme Regis
Dorset DT7 3LS
Tel: 01297-443948
Fax: 01297-442722
e-mail: help@russellhouse.co.uk
www.russellhouse.co.uk

© Neil Thompson

British Library Cataloguing-in-publication Data:

A catalogue record for this book is available from the British Library.

ISBN: 978-1-903855-99-7

Typeset by TW Typesetting, Plymouth, Devon
Printed by Alden, Oxford

## About Russell House Publishing

Russell House Publishing aims to publish innovative and valuable materials to help managers, practitioners, trainers, educators and students.

Our full catalogue covers: social policy, working with young people, helping children and families, care of older people, social care, combating social exclusion, revitalising communities and working with offenders.

Full details can be found at www.russellhouse.co.uk and we are pleased to send out information to you by post. Our contact details are on this page.

We are always keen to receive feedback on publications and new ideas for future projects.

# Contents

# The Theory into Practice Series

This exciting new series fills a significant gap in the market for short, user-friendly texts, written by experts, that succinctly introduce sets of theoretical ideas, relate them clearly to practice issues, and guide the reader to further learning. They particularly address discrimination, oppression, equality and diversity. They can be read either as general overviews of particular areas of theory and practice, or as foundations for further study. The series will be invaluable across the human services, including social work and social care; youth and community work; criminal and community justice work; counselling; advice work; housing; and aspects of health care.

## About the Series Editor

**Neil Thompson** is a Director of Avenue Consulting Ltd (www.avenueconsulting.co.uk), a company offering training and consultancy in relation to social work and human relations issues. He is also Professor of of Social Work and Well-being at Liverpool Hope University. He has over 100 publications to his name, including best-selling textbooks, papers in scholarly journals and training and open learning materials.

Neil is a Fellow of the Chartered Institute of Personnel and Development, the Institute of Training and Occupational Learning and the Royal Society of Arts (elected on the basis of his contribution to organisational learning). He was the founding editor of the *British Journal of Occupational Learning* (www.trainingin-stitute.co.uk). He was also responsible for the setting up of the self-help website, www.humansolutions.org.uk and the Social Well-being blog: http://socialwell-being.blogspot.com. His personal website is at www.neilthompson.info.

# Series Editor's Foreword

## About the series

The relationship between theory and practice is one that has puzzled practitioners and theorists alike for some considerable time, and there still remains considerable debate about how the two interconnect. However, what is clear is that it is dangerous to tackle the complex problems encountered in 'people work' without having at least a basic understanding of what makes people tick, of how the social context plays a part in both the problems we address and the solutions we seek. Working with people and their problems is difficult and demanding work. To try to undertake it without being armed with a sound professional knowledge base is a very risky strategy indeed, and potentially a disastrous one.

An approach to practice based mainly on guesswork, untested assumptions, habit and copying others is clearly not one that can be supported. Good practice must be an *informed* practice, with actions based, as far as possible, on reasoning, understanding and evidence. This series is intended to develop just such good practice by providing:

- an introductory overview of a particular area of theory or professional knowledge;
- an exploration of how it relates to practice issues;
- a consideration of how the theory base can help tackle discrimination and oppression; and
- a guide to further learning.

The texts in the series are written by people with extensive knowledge and practical experience in the fields concerned and are intended as an introduction to the wider and more in-depth literature base.

## About this book

This particular text, with its focus on power and empowerment, provides an important discussion of some highly significant issues that have a broad application across a wide variety of work settings that involve dealing with people and their problems. It is concerned with two inter-related topics, and both are unfortunately very prone to oversimplification. Given that this is a short, introductory textbook, it is very important to make sure that it does not add to the tendency to oversimplify. The book's aims must therefore be quite modest. No author could possibly say all there is to say about power in a single book, even if it were a huge tome, and so this short book must limit itself to providing an introductory overview of some of the main theoretical issues (Part One); exploring some of the practice implications (Part Two); identifying important issues relating to tackling discrimination and oppression (Part Three); and providing suggestions for further learning (Part Four).

It is to be hoped that the book will (i) provide a helpful introduction to some of the complexities of this subject area; (ii) establish the dangers of neglecting or oversimplifying the issues involved; (iii) provide some insights about how power and empowerment can and should be managed in practice; (iv) establish a platform for future debate, study and learning; and (v) instil a degree of enthusiasm for developing a broader and deeper understanding of power, empowerment and related matters.

**Neil Thompson, Series Editor**

*For Tom and Gabrielle*

# About the author

**Neil Thompson** is an independent consultant, trainer and author with Avenue Consulting Ltd and Professor of Social Work and Well-being at Liverpool Hope University. His interests include equality and diversity; workplace well-being; loss and grief; and workplace learning. He is a well-published author and his recent books include *People Problems* (Palgrave Macmillan, 2006a) and *Promoting Workplace Learning* (The Policy Press, 2006b).

Neil has a long-standing commitment to promoting equality and social justice. This book is the result of, and a contribution to, that commitment.

# Acknowledgements

Several people have been helpful in the development of this book. I am very grateful to John Bates of Liverpool Hope University, Bernard Moss of Staffordshire University and Graham Thompson of the University of Wales Bangor for their comments on an earlier draft. I am also indebted to Professor Julienne Meyer of City University, Professor Mark Doel of Sheffield Hallam University and Dr Julian Buchanan of North East Wales Institute for their kind comments about the value of the book.

As always, Susan Thompson is another person whose support has been invaluable in so many ways.

Finally, I would also like to thank Geoffrey Mann at the publishers for his continued support and friendship.

# Introduction

Morriss (2002, p. 1) sets the scene nicely for this book when he argues that:

> The meaning of the word 'power' seems like a will-o'-the-wisp: it tends to dissolve entirely whenever we look at it closely. We are sure that we meant *something* by the word, and have a vague idea what it is: but this understanding tends to fade away upon examination, until 'power' seems nothing more than 'a giant glob of oily ambiguity' (Dahl, 1957b: p. 1056).

Of course, power is much more than a 'giant glob of oily ambiguity', but the point is well made that it is not an easy concept to pin down. Indeed, it is one that we need to wrestle with, rather than something that can be easily defined and neatly 'packaged'. When we come to the related concept of empowerment, we find an equally tricky concept and another one that does not lend itself to a simple treatment. Indeed, as we shall see, both power and empowerment are concepts that have been dogged by a very strong tendency to oversimplification (or, to use the technical term, 'reductionism'). The complex, multi-level nature of both has tended to be reduced to the dangerously distorted level of 'sound bites' – leading to not only a great deal of confusion, but also a certain amount of ill-feeling, as many people have been alienated by clumsy, unsophisticated and simplistic approaches that can do more harm than good. A key aim of this book, then, is to paint a picture of how complex the territory is and to provide some degree of guidance on how to navigate it.

Like other books in the *Theory into Practice* series, this text is divided into four parts. In Part One I provide a discussion first of the theory base relating to power and then the theory base relating to empowerment. Part Two builds on this by exploring some of the practice implications of both power and empowerment. Part Three links our two key concepts to various aspects of discrimination and provides a basis for promoting equality and valuing diversity. Part Four is a 'guide to further learning' and includes suggestions for further reading and details of relevant organisations and websites.

To provide an overview of the theory base relating to power and empowerment and link it to practice in general and anti-discriminatory practice in particular in one short text is clearly an ambitious undertaking. However, what makes it a realistic undertaking is that it is a matter of producing a 'gateway' text – that is, one that provides just enough information to lay a foundation for further study and learning. This book, then, should not be seen as a complete learning experience in its own right, but, rather, as the beginning of a longer and broader learning process that should allow you to develop your understanding further.

The subject matter of this book is both highly complex and very important. It is therefore doubly important that you should see what is offered here as part of a wider whole, rather than a finished product in its own right: (i) to do justice to the complexities involved; and (ii) to recognise how significant both power and empowerment are in any form of 'people work' – that is, occupations that are involved in working with people and helping them tackle the problems they encounter.

I hope you will find that what is offered in the pages that follow is informative, stimulating and helpful. It is not intended to provide all the answers, but it should provide you with a foundation from which to continue learning, so that you can develop your own answers to each of the challenges that power and empowerment will continue to cast before us.

# Part One: Power and Empowerment Theory

## Introduction

---

Part One is the first of four parts of the book. It is concerned with laying down the foundations for developing a fuller understanding of power and empowerment. As such, it presents an introduction to some of the key concepts and issues that have informed our understanding of power and empowerment up to now. What I have to say on the subject is far from definitive, as this is a contested area of social theory – that is, it is a field characterised by a large number of debates and disagreements. However, it is to be hoped that what is presented will offer considerable food for thought and important insights to guide practice and future learning.

Part One is divided into two chapters. In the first I present an overview of the theory base relating to power and, in doing so, explain a number of important ideas. In the second I discuss the closely related topic of empowerment, again explaining some of the most important concepts that relate to it. These are both huge topics, and so what is presented here will necessarily be selective and far from comprehensive. The subject matter is also very complex and, while I have tried to present the ideas as clearly as possible, they remain intellectually quite challenging. You may therefore find it helpful to come back to Part One and re-read it after you have read the other three parts of the book.

This first part of the book sets the scene for Part Two in which some of the main practice implications of the theory base are explored. Consistent with the ethos of the *Theory into Practice* series, the aim is to link theory and practice together, rather than present them as separate entities with little or no connection.

# Chapter 1
# Power

In this chapter I explore some of the key issues relating to the theory base underpinning the notion of power. I begin by asking the important question: What is power? This then sets the scene for a discussion of some important concepts that are part of the extensive theory base that is not only important for our understanding of power, but also significant in making sense of empowerment, a topic we shall examine in some detail in Chapter 2.

Everyone has some degree of power, but, of course, some people are in stronger positions than others – society is not a level playing field. We can therefore see that there are strong links between power issues and matters relating to equality and diversity. These links will be explored in Part Three.

---

### Exercise 1.1

Before reading on, pause for a moment and think about what the word 'power' means to you. What does the word conjure up in your mind? What do you associate it with? Bear your answers in mind as you continue your reading.

---

## What is power?

It is important to begin by recognising that power is a term that is widely used, but none the less very difficult to pin down. It is a theoretical concept, and is therefore understood differently within different theoretical perspectives. This means that it would be difficult, if not impossible, to pin down one agreed definition. We will need to settle for a broader understanding of the term that takes account of different theoretical orientations towards it.

Consequently, my task here is not to provide a definitive answer to the various debates about power, but rather to explore what the different conceptions are and what implications they have for practice and management in the human services. First of all, it is important to recognise that power is a term used in a variety of senses. We need to clarify that we are interested here in power in the social sense – that is, excluding power in the sense of energy, such as electricity (the power supply) or wind power; and the power of music or art, and so on. However, there are connections to be made between these forms of power and the social forms of power that occupy our attention here – albeit at a more advanced level than would be appropriate in an introductory book such as this.

In trying to appreciate the complexities of the subject, we can identify different models of power, not least the following:

### Psychological or personal

Psychological models of power are concerned with an individual's ability to achieve his or her own ends. This involves:

- *Skills* Communication, assertiveness, influence, and so on.
- *Attributes* Sexual attractiveness, parental or other such status, respect, charisma, and so on.
- *Role* Manager, inspector, assessor, and so on.
- *Attitudes* Confidence, self-belief, willingness to take risks, and so on.

We shall discuss some of these concepts in more detail below, in particular that of charisma. One further point to note at this juncture is that skills can be learned, while attributes are assigned or acquired over time. Similarly, roles are partly learned and partly assigned or acquired, and the same can be said of attitudes: they are a combination of what is learned and how we respond to others and how they respond to us.

### Discursive or cultural

This relates in large part to Foucault's notion of discourse, the capacity of language to create structures of power. This is a concept that we shall discuss in more detail and develop more fully below.

A discourse is literally a conversation, but it is used to refer to frameworks of language, meaning and behaviour that contain within them certain 'power rules', as it were. For example, in what is known as medical discourse, we have the notion of 'doctor's orders' – that is, the assumption that patients are obliged to follow the instructions of doctors when there is, in fact, no such legal requirement. This is an example of how the discourse surrounding medicine gives great power to doctors. Hugman (1991) captures the point well in the following passage:

> Discourse is about more than language. Discourse is about the interplay between language and social relationships, in which some groups are able to achieve dominance for their interests in the way in which the world is defined and acted upon. Such groups include not only dominant economic classes, but also men within patriarchy, and white people within the racism of colonial and post-colonial societies (Fanon, 1967; Spender, 1980), as well as professionals in relation to service users. Language is a central aspect of discourse through which power is reproduced and communicated. (p. 37)

Discourses become a part of culture, in so far as they shape the taken-for-granted assumptions and unwritten rules that are such an important part of cultural formations. As we shall see below, much power derives from this cultural level.

Discourses in particular and cultures in general steer us in certain directions and therefore away from others. This in itself is a very significant exercise of power. Discourses in effect construct reality. Within a discourse is the power to define – for example, to define what is normal (as opposed to abnormal) and what is acceptable. We shall return to these models below when we discuss 'Theorising power'.

The cultural level is connected to the personal level, in so far as 'one's subjectivity is produced through discourses' (Healy, 2000, p. 45) – that is, a person's identity is in part formed through cultural or discursive processes.

### *Structural*

This refers to a person's location in the social hierarchy along various dimensions, such as class, race, ethnicity, gender, and so on. These are the main ones that are generally recognised, but it is important not to forget that there are other structural factors that have a bearing. These include age, disability, sexual identity, religion and language.

The structural dimension of power applies in a number of ways:

- *Access to resources* This is a matter of 'financial clout'. For example, some people have the power to buy the best educational or health care facilities available, while people at the lower end of the financial spectrum have to make do with what is available to them from state resources.
- *Ideological assumptions* This is a matter of 'hegemony', a concept we shall discuss in more detail below. An example of this would be the notion of white supremacy, the worrying, but sadly not uncommon, assumption amongst many people that white people are inherently superior to black people.
- *Barriers* Many of the barriers to progress are of a structural nature – for example, the well-documented 'glass ceiling' that seems to operate to reduce the number of women in senior management positions.

An important concept that connects the structural level to the cultural level is that of 'autopoiesis' (see Thompson, 2003a). This is a process through which structures and related cultural formations reproduce themselves over time. For example, in a male-dominated management team, a male applicant for a post within that team is likely to come across more favourably in terms of the required qualities, as compared with a female applicant whose strengths may not be appreciated within that culture. This links to Becker's (1967) notion of 'a hierarchy of credibility' – that is, the notion that the higher up a person is within a particular hierarchy (or power structure), the more likely it is that he or she will be listened to.

Power, then, can be understood to operate at these three levels: personal, cultural and structural. It is not a case of trying to establish which is the 'correct' or 'true' level at which power operates but, rather, to appreciate that it is to be found at all three of these levels. This is an example of the complexity of power that has not always been acknowledged or understood.

A further example of this trend towards oversimplification is the tendency to assign people to one of two basic categories, powerful or powerless. Fook (2002) explains this well when she argues that:

> People do not fit easily into 'powerful' or 'powerless' groupings, sometimes having membership of both at the same time. As well, members of powerless groups do not necessarily agree on the form of their empowerment. Some people may experience the very same experience as empowering and others as disempowering. Sometimes what is empowering for some might actually detract from the empowerment of others. (p. 47)

The tendency to think in simplistic, black and white terms (seeing people as either powerful or powerless) is an example of 'reductionism', reducing a complex, multi-level phenomenon to a single level. It is a common mistake in theoretical analysis and in efforts to relate theory to practice. The discussions below should show how significant an error this can be.

A further example of oversimplification is the common, but misguided assumption that power is necessarily a bad thing, always a negative force. Westwood's (2002) comments in relation to the work of Foucault (1978) on this matter are instructive:

> Following Nietzsche (1844–1900), Foucault (1926–84) regards power not as negative or positive but as omnipresent and productive. However, there are different forms of power, from governance through state organisations and the management of populations to discipline through internal bureaucracies and institutional arrangements that come to bear on all citizens in modern societies. (p. 19)

Power can do harm, but it can also do good. This will be an important theme when we discuss empowerment, as this clearly involves drawing on the positive elements of power, including the various forms of power Foucault mentions. If power were necessarily a bad thing, why would we want to support empowerment? Clearly, a simplistic, one-sided view of power that sees only the negatives is not sufficient to do justice to this complex subject.

---

### Practice Focus 1.1

Lin had become very confused about the subject of power. She had come to believe that power was a significant problem, because so many of the problems she encountered in her work were as a result of unequal power relations. If power is such a problem, how does it make sense to want to empower people? However, after discussing this with Glenys, her supervisor, the cloud of confusion lifted. Glenys had pointed out to her that it is not power itself that is a problem, it is when such power has the result of some people being disadvantaged or oppressed in some way. Power, she went on to explain, has the potential to do harm, but it is important not to oversimplify by assuming that power is always a problem or source of problems.

---

### Exercise 1.2

In what ways can power be used positively? What examples can you identify? What implications might this have for your work?

---

So, what is power, then? Just as it can be seen to operate at three levels (personal, cultural and structural), it can also be defined in three ways: dispositional, discursive and structural. Let us explore each of these in turn.

## Power as disposition

Power can be understood as a 'disposition', a capability we have. Dowding (1996) offers apt comment in this regard:

> Power is a dispositional concept. To say that I have the power to throw a stone 50 metres is to say that I *could* throw that stone 50 metres, not that I *am* throwing it that far. It is to say that I have the capacity to throw it. (p. 3)

A good example of power as a disposition is 'charisma'. This refers to the personality characteristics and skills that particular individuals can possess which enable them to be very effective in influencing others. Major political leaders, such as Gandhi and Churchill are generally quoted as 'charismatic' leaders. However, it is not only famous people or politicians who can be described as charismatic. Managers and professionals in the human services can also have charismatic qualities, as indeed can any member of the public. Some people may have charismatic qualities, but may not draw on them. This is an example of power as a 'disposition' – the capacity to exercise power exists, but it is not necessarily used.

## Power as institutionalised ideas and practices

This relates to the work of Foucault, as mentioned earlier. Ideas and practices become firmly established within 'discourses' or frameworks of meaning and social practices. They thus become 'institutionalised' – so firmly ingrained through constant repetition and use within a particular culture or social setting that they become very powerful influences, taken for granted as normal or 'natural'.

The notion of 'hegemony' is very relevant here. Westwood (2002) comments as follows:

Gramsci understood the power of culture as lived practices, and the ways in which power blocs from the ruling classes could generate a consensus in society through the processes of ideological hegemony. This did not mean simply that people were duped, but that the ideological spaces were both actively embraced and resisted by people in relation to a vast array of messages and signs mediated by the life circumstances of individuals. (p. 13)

This is an important passage that is worth exploring in more detail:

- *The power of culture as lived practices* This captures the idea that cultures develop powerful sets of practices that become people's everyday realities – for example, the sexual division of labour (the tendency for some jobs to be seen as 'men's work' while others are seen typically as 'women's work').
- *Generating a consensus* This is what makes cultures so powerful: they involve developing discourses that are accepted as a social consensus. For example, the idea that children should not be involved in sexual behaviour is widely accepted, even though different societies have different definitions of what constitutes an appropriate 'age of consent' (12 in the Netherlands, for example). This is not to say that children *should* be involved in sexual activity, but rather simply to state that the idea that they should not has become so firmly established as to constitute a social consensus. That is, there will be relatively few people who disagree and they are likely to be labelled as 'deviant' for doing so.
- *Ideological hegemony* Ideology is the power of ideas, and hegemony is the ability of ideas to become so strongly accepted that they become dominant (hegemony means 'dominance', but dominance through the acceptance of ideas, not through force or other such pressures).
- *Embracing ideological spaces* This is how hegemony works. The dominant ideas of a society are 'embraced' by people, rather than forced upon them. This is what makes the ideas so powerful – the fact that they become established as normal or even 'natural'. For example, same-sex relationships are often presented as 'unnatural', as if to imply that they 'go against' biology. The fact that homosexuality was for many years officially classified as a mental illness is a clear illustration of this.
- *Resisting ideological spaces* Although dominant ideas do tend to be embraced (and that is what actually makes them dominant), there is also much resistance to them – for example, movements that challenge dominant notions, such as the women's movement challenging discourses about gender that place women in inferior positions relative to men.
- *Vast array of messages and signs* The 'cultural transmission' of discourses occurs through communication in general and the media in particular, and so 'messages and signs' are an important part of this.
- *Mediated by the life circumstances of individuals* We are not, though, simply puppets carried along by the forces of discourse – our life circumstances,

including the choices we make and the actions we take, can also be important factors in the equation.

Clearly, then, power is much more complex than one or more dispositions. Our understanding of it must therefore go beyond the individual or personal level.

### Power as structural relations

The development of conceptions of power concerned with discourses and institutionalised patterns of language and behaviour was in part a reaction against approaches that emphasised the importance of structural factors. It is partly for this reason that the work of Foucault and others who adopt similar approaches is described as 'poststructuralism'. However, it would be a mistake to remove the structural dimension from the picture. As we shall see, it has an important part to play.

Society is divided up into different social sectors – for example, in terms of class, gender and race/ethnicity. The key point to note is that such groupings are not 'on a level playing field' – that is, there is a power hierarchy implicit within the social structure. This leads to a set of profound social inequalities – for example in terms of health. The Department of Health (1998) shows that differences in life expectancy between people in the highest and lowest income groups are quite marked. Experiences of ill health follow a similar pattern of structured inequality.

Russell (2004, p. 165) makes the important point that government, as a welcome alternative to anarchy and despotism, necessarily involves some degree of inequality of power. However, unequal power relations should not be equated with oppression. Rather, it is the (deliberate) abuse or (unwitting) misuse of power that should be recognised as the basis of oppression (Thompson, 2003a). As with power as a disposition, structural relations offer the *potential* for oppression, but simply having a hierarchy is not necessarily oppressive. This is a very complex issue, and so it is important not to oversimplify it by making the reductionist assumption that social structures are necessarily oppressive (see Part Four for guidance on further reading on these issues).

A key matter here is the concept of 'authority', which can be defined as the *legitimate* use of power. For example, having a police force which exercises power is not oppressive in itself, as the safeguarding of law and order is generally regarded as socially legitimate. Oppression would arise, for example, where such power is used unfairly or disproportionately. This is an important issue for human services professionals and managers, as it highlights the potential for positions of authority to be abused or misused – and this is a very good reason why we need to have at least a basic understanding of power and how it works.

---

**Exercise 1.3**

What structural factors are relevant to your area of work? What implications might these have for your practice?

---

## A multi-level analysis: structuration theory and beyond

Traditionally the different conceptions of power have arisen from different schools of thought. For example, dispositional and personal-level accounts are associated with psychology and philosophy, while institutionalised practices approaches are associated with poststructuralist thinking in such subjects as sociology and anthropology, and structural understandings are connected with marxist thinking in sociology, economics and politics. Because of this, they have tended to occupy different theoretical and practical spaces, with relatively little attempt to unify their insights into a coherent whole. To establish such a unification would be a theoretical task of major proportions, but for present purposes, we can see that our understanding of power will be better served if we take account of all three levels or dimensions, rather than stick to one or even two.

Individualist dispositional accounts can be criticised for not taking sufficient account of the social circumstances in which power operates (that is, they treat power as a psychological concept and thus neglect the sociological aspects, rather than recognising it as a phenomenon that has both psychological and sociological dimensions). The poststructuralist approach introduces a sociological dimension, but, as Westwood (2002) points out: 'Habermas criticises Foucault's work because collectivities in struggle are absent from the analysis' (p. 17). In other words, it neglects the structural dimension. In turn, the structural approach can be criticised for focusing too exclusively on structures and not enough on other aspects. That is, it presents what many people would refer to as a 'monolithic' understanding of power.

One approach that has sought to bring personal and structural aspects together is structuration theory. 'Structuration' is a concept that has been developed by leading sociologist, Anthony Giddens. It refers to the way in which agency (my actions, for example) interact with the wider social structure (the context of my actions). Giddens's theory is geared towards explaining how human existence is characterised by the interplay of these two important sets of factors. It is not simply the case that we have free will and can do precisely what we like, as that is a naïve approach that fails to take account of the constraints of wider social factors. However, we should also not go to the opposite unhelpful extreme of assuming that wider social structural factors *determine* what happens to us without our having a say in the matter whatsoever. The reality of the situation is a complex dialectical interplay between agency and structure, between our actions (agency) and the context of those actions (structure).

As I have argued previously (Thompson, 2003a), structuration theory has considerable strengths, but one weakness within it is that it pays little or no attention to the cultural level, the level of shared meanings, taken-for-granted assumptions, unwritten rules, and so on (although some aspects of what Giddens describes as 'structure' have much in common with the cultural level – see Stones, 2005). If we are to understand empowerment, we must recognise the interplay not only of agency (the personal level) and the structural level, but also interactions between agency and the cultural level (and, indeed, between the cultural and structural levels). This adds up to a very complex picture of social reality. However, we need to have this level of complexity if we are to do justice to the intricacies of empowerment.

In some respects, structuration theory has much in common with existentialism. A key concept within existentialism is the idea that existential freedom (the ability and indeed requirement to choose) is a necessary precursor to political liberty. In other words, if we deny human agency, then political liberty becomes impossible. We cannot achieve broader political freedoms if we deny that we have some degree of control (and therefore responsibility) over our actions. Clearly, then, agency is an essential concept when it comes to developing a theoretical understanding of power and, indeed, of empowerment.

Power, then, is not a simple matter. It has different levels and dimensions and, while much theorising of this area has been done over the years, there is still much more to be done before we can feel that we have a sound understanding of the complexities. In the meantime, however, it can be useful to review the theoretical knowledge we do have, and it is to this that we now turn.

## Theorising power

It is certainly beyond the scope of this book to present a comprehensive analysis of the theoretical underpinnings of power as currently conceived. A more realistic goal is to review some of the key issues and consider, albeit briefly, their significance for professional practice and management.

### Power as sociological: Lukes

The point has already been made that it is important to incorporate a sociological understanding of power and not rely simply on a narrow psychological perspective. One writer whose work on power emphasises the sociological dimension is Steven Lukes who wrote a classic text, published originally in 1974, with an expanded and updated edition published in 2005. His work is also concerned with three dimensions, but this time in terms of *views of* power, rather than power itself:

- *One-dimensional view of power* This refers to the power involved in, for example, decision making. It is concerned with the behaviour involved in reaching decisions in situations involving conflict – that is, the power of one person or group to achieve their ends, possibly contrary to the interests of others.
- *Two-dimensional view of power* In this view of power, there is a concern with not only decision making, but also 'non-decision making' – the power to set the agenda and thus also to suppress items from appearing on that agenda.
- *Three-dimensional view of power* This refers to the significance of the social context. Lukes describes how social patterns create a set of power relations:

> the bias of the system is not sustained simply by a series of individually chosen acts, but also, most importantly, by the socially structured and culturally patterned behaviour of groups, and practices of institutions, which may indeed be manifested by individuals' inaction. (2005, p. 26)

This is close to the 'institutionalised practices' approach associated with Foucault in so far as it recognises that power arises in part from repeated patterns of behaviour and language use that then become established as the norm (with deviations from that norm being socially disapproved of). It also reflects elements of the structural approach by acknowledging the role of social structures in creating and maintaining relations of power.

Lukes's work has helped broaden out our understanding of power by exploring the sociological dimensions involved.

---

### Practice Focus 1.2

When Ram attended a training course on empowerment, he felt that too much emphasis was being placed on what he referred to as 'so-called male power'. He pointed out to the trainer that his boss was a woman, the most powerful person in his family was his mother and, as a black man in a white-dominated society, he could not see himself as 'a powerful male', and therefore found the idea of male dominance a hard one to accept. However, the trainer helped him to look at the situation more broadly, to see the sociological picture and, while his comments about his own life experiences were perfectly valid, these had to be seen in the context of a society where power is far more closely associated with men than women. The trainer also explained how power is very complex and that the overall theme of male dominance had to be set in context alongside some of the things he had mentioned: power relating to race relations, the power involved in family dynamics and so on. Ram was beginning to appreciate that power is a very complex matter and that he would need to take more account of the wider (sociological) picture as well as his own direct experience.

### 'Power to' and 'power over'

A long-standing distinction made in the literature relating to power is that between 'power to' and 'power over'. 'Power to' equates with the individual, dispositional model of power. It refers to a person's potential to achieve their ends. The Latin verb, 'potere', which means 'to be able' can be seen as its root and is connected with the word, 'potential'. To have power is therefore to have the potential (to achieve our ends). In this way, empowerment amounts to realising one's potential and is therefore an important issue for human services practice and, indeed for management more broadly.

By contrast, 'power over' refers to how power can be used to dominate, to produce a relationship of subordination. This can be at a personal level – for example, where a relationship between two people is not one of equals, but where one dominates the other. It can also be at a structural level – for example, where men (as a social group) occupy positions of power in relation to women (as a social group). Confusion between the personal and structural levels has led to many problems over the years. An example of this would be many people assuming that, because men at a structural level can be seen to be in a position of dominance (in terms of occupying positions of power), individual men are necessarily more powerful than individual women. This is clearly a mistaken assumption. Consider, for example, the case of the power relations between a female managing director of a company in relation to a male junior employee. This is not to say that structural gender relations will not play a part. For example, the female managing director may have faced all sorts of obstacles in her rise to the top that a male may not have. Again we are dealing with complex issues and it is clearly not enough to rely on a reductionist notion of 'men are powerful, women are not'.

'Power over' is also relevant at a cultural level. This is because the dominant ideas that are part and parcel of cultural assumptions and practices are, as Marx pointed out long ago, the ideas of dominant groups. In other words, structural relations of dominance are reinforced by cultural assumptions: patriarchal power structures are supported and reinforced by patriarchal cultural assumptions and indeed discourses.

An understanding of power based in the concept of discourse involves elements of both 'power to' and 'power over', but does not take full account of either, hence the need to understand, and take account of, all three levels.

---

#### Exercise 1.4

Can you identify any discourses relating to your area of work (that is, established frameworks of language, meaning and practice that are powerful influences on what is seen as 'normal' or 'acceptable')?

The two forms (or 'species' as Lukes calls them) of power are not entirely separate. As Dowding (1996) explains:

> Now 'power over' implies 'power to', for A will have power over B to make B do X. A has the power to make B do it. 'Power to' and 'power over' may be described as 'outcome power' and 'social power' respectively, the first because it is the power to bring about outcomes, the second because it necessarily involves a social relation between at least two actors (Dowding 1991: 48). We may give a formal definition of these two concepts:
>
> outcome power = the ability of an actor to bring about or help to bring about outcomes
>
> social power = the ability of an actor deliberately to change the incentive structure of another actor or actors to bring about or help to bring about outcomes (pp. 4–5)

This distinction between 'power to' and 'power over' is important because it shows the importance of dominance as a social phenomenon, but also shows that power is not necessarily dominance.

### *'Power with' and 'power from within': Rowlands*

While we have seen that the distinction between 'power to' and 'power over' is a significant and useful one, Rowlands (1998), in discussing the empowerment of women, adds a further two very significant elements:

> Men's fear of losing control is an obstacle to women's empowerment, but is it necessarily an outcome of women's empowerment that men should lose power or, crucially that a loss of power should be something to be afraid of? With a 'power over' view of power, it is hard to imagine otherwise.
>
> There are, however, other ways of understanding and conceptualising power, which focus not just on a particular set of results but on *process*. Power can take other forms, variously described as 'power to', 'power with' and 'power from within', all of which allow the construction of a very different meaning (or set of meanings) for 'empowerment'. (p. 13)

Rowlands (1998) goes on to explain 'power with' in the following terms:

> Some analysts also identify 'power with', which 'involves a sense of the whole being greater than the sum of the individuals, especially when a group tackles problems together' (quoted in Williams *et al.*, 1995: 234). (p. 14)

This is an important concept in terms of empowerment, as it helps to establish that working together collaboratively can be a useful way forward. This can be seen to apply in two ways. First, people in disadavantaged positions can work collectively to pursue their goals – that is, they can find that their concerted, collective power is much greater than isolated efforts to bring about change (strength in unity). It is therefore important to think of empowerment as more than simply an individual or personal matter. Second, it means that, when it comes to professional involvement, it is better to work collaboratively – that is, in partnership – rather than in a top-down 'we know best' way. This will prove to be an important issue in both Chapter 4 and Chapter 6.

Rowlands (1998) is also helpful in explaining that:

> There is also 'power from within', 'the spiritual strength and uniqueness that resides in each one of us and makes us truly human. Its basis is self-acceptance and self-respect, which extend, in turn, to respect for and acceptance of others as equals' (ibid). This power can be what enables the individual to hold a position or activity in the face of overwhelming opposition, or to take a serious risk. (p. 14)

Many people who adopt a fairly hard-headed sociological understanding of power would perhaps baulk at this spirituality-oriented dimension of power. However, there is no reason why spirituality, in the sense of meaning making and finding one's place in the wider world (Moss, 2005), cannot be very relevant to issues of power and empowerment and compatible with sociology (phenomenological or existentialist approaches to sociology in particular – see, for example, Craib, 1976).

---

**Practice Focus 1.3**

Steph was used to helping people get through very difficult times in their lives. However, when she had two significant bereavements in her own life, plus other serious family problems, she was really concerned that she was not going to be able to cope. She recognised the irony that she might 'go under' in her own struggle to deal with immense difficulties after having helped so many others to cope.

The turning point came for her when she felt 'close to the edge' and somehow managed to find the resources from within to make sure she got through. This 'power from within' gave her the impetus to link together with other family members to draw on 'power with' to support one another through these extremely challenging times.

---

The notion of 'power from within' links well with the existentialist concept of authenticity which can be defined as follows:

> Authenticity involves being able to recognize the boundary between those aspects of our lives that we can control and those that we cannot, and making sure that what belongs in the first category does not get assigned to the second. (Thompson, 2005a, p. 127)

Indeed, authenticity can be seen as very relevant to empowerment more broadly:

> Empowerment is often a matter of helping people remove barriers to progress – and authenticity has a part to play in this, as so often many of the barriers we face are

partly self-made (for example, a person may lack confidence as a result of having internalized comments made by teachers and others that he or she was of low ability. Some forms of . . . [practice] can be helpful in constructively confronting and undermining such barriers – helping people to help themselves. (*ibid.*)

The four 'species' of power can therefore be summarised as follows:

- *Power to* This type of power is concerned with people's ability to achieve their goals. From a professional point of view, this can be seen to be a foundation for maximising potential – for example, by helping people recognise and tackle any obstacles to developing their potential.
- *Power over* This is used to describe unequal power relations – that is, relations of dominance. Where this occurs in a way that is seen as socially legitimate (child protection, for example), it is recognised as the exercise of authority. When relations of dominance occur that are not socially legitimate (racism, for example), or where legitimate authority is abused or misused (unnecessary use of force by police officers, for example), this amounts to oppression.
- *Power with* This is the basis of partnership and a collective approach. By working together and encouraging others to work together, more can be achieved than by working in isolation or at odds with one another.
- *Power from within* Power is closely associated in some ways with the notion of resources, and that includes personal or inner resources. Power from within therefore refers to the strength and resilience we can draw upon and help others to draw upon. It is therefore closely associated with notions of spirituality (finding meaning, direction and connection in our lives) and authenticity (avoiding self-deception).

### Power and knowledge

The idea that 'knowledge is power' is a well established one. However, the relationship between power and knowledge amounts to much more than this. This is because knowledge is developed within discourses which in themselves are sites of power, as we noted earlier. Turner (1995) makes apt comment when he argues that:

> We should admit . . . that power produces knowledge . . . that power and knowledge directly imply one another; that there is no power relation without the correlative constitution of a field of knowledge, nor any knowledge that does not presuppose and constitute at the same time power relations. These 'power-knowledge' relations are to be analysed, therefore, not on the basis of a subject of knowledge who is or is not free in relation to the power system, but on the contrary, the subject who knows, the objects to be known and the modalities of knowledge must be regarded as so many effects of these fundamental implications of power knowledge and their historical transformations (Foucault, 1977: 27–8). (p. 12)

This has implications in terms of how knowledge is used in professional practice. For example, developing a knowledge base of mental health problems based on a medicalised conception of the subject has consequences for how the identified problems are dealt with. As we shall see in Chapter 2, this can have (detrimental) implications when it comes to promoting empowerment. This is because a medical model approach has the effect of 'pathologising' the individual concerned (that is, presenting the problems as a deficiency within the person) and distracting attention from the wider factors.

How professional knowledge is developed and how it is used therefore have significant implications in relation to power and thus empowerment.

### The power of language

The relationship between power and language is a complex one. This is because:

- *Language reflects power relations* An example of this is the use of gender-related terminology in ways that give a clear message of male dominance: 'The reader must make his own mind up about whether masculine forms of language place women in a position of subordination'.
- *Language reinforces power relations* As we have noted, patterns of language use that become institutionalised through repetition form 'discourses' that contain within them powerful messages about what is normal, natural and acceptable (and thus what is abnormal, unnatural and unacceptable).

Unfortunately, the topic of language and power has been subject to considerable oversimplification (see the discussion of 'political correctness' in Thompson, 2003b). It is not simply a case of banning certain words and using others in their place. What is needed is a far more sophisticated understanding of how language and power interrelate.

### Power and conflict

Conflict is an everyday part of human services practice and management (albeit often at a low level) and, indeed, it is a key skill to be able to manage conflict effectively. This involves being able to use 'power to' and, to a certain extent, 'power over', but in such ways as not to alienate the people involved and thus risk an escalation of the conflict. In effect, the negotiation and assertiveness skills involved in conflict management can be seen to amount to skills in the sensitive and appropriate use of power.

In addition, conflict can be seen to arise as a result of the exercise of power. For example, one person exercising their power can lead to problems for one or more other persons exercising their power, hence they enter into conflict. Developing our understanding of power can therefore help us to enhance our understanding of conflict and its significance in human services practice and management.

### Power and powerlessness

In considering power, we also need to take account of powerlessness. While we can all experience powerlessness at times, certain groups can be seen to be particularly prone to powerlessness:

- *people with mental health problems* This can be seen to arise as a result of the combination of the debilitating effects of their condition and the consequences of medicalisation (Laurance, 2003), as well as discrimination;
- *people with learning disabilities* There is a strong parallel here with mental health problems, although the medicalisation of learning disabilities is arguably less pronounced (but none the less sufficient to be problematic);
- *people with physical disabilities* The same pattern can be seen to apply here, with a particularly strong focus on discrimination, based predominantly on stereotypes of disability;
- *people with long-term illnesses* Illness itself, whether long or short term, can be disempowering, but discrimination can add to this, especially where the illness is socially disapproved of (AIDS, for example);
- *children (especially looked-after children)* There is a growing recognition that children should be given greater voice, in acknowledgement of their relative powerlessness;
- *older people* Traditional approaches to work with older people have assumed that it is natural for them to 'disengage' from society. Such ageist assumptions have contributed to their occupying a marginalised (and thus relatively powerless) position;
- *homeless people* Being homeless brings not only the direct problems of lacking shelter and 'roots', but also a degree of discrimination and stigma, as well as political disenfranchisement to a certain extent; and
- *ex-offenders* Stigma and discrimination also apply to ex-offenders – ironically potentially leading to a higher reliance on criminal activity.

We also need to recognise that these categories will 'cross cut' with one another. That is, an ex-offender may have mental health problems and be homeless, thus encountering an accumulation of problems. Furthermore, these categories will 'cross cut' with class, race, gender and so on, thus providing further potential for multiple oppression and extreme powerlessness. We should therefore bear in mind, when dealing with people in those categories of people who are likely to be more vulnerable to powerlessness, that the reality is likely to be far more complex and intricate than reductionist accounts of power and powerlessness would lead us to believe.

---

### Exercise 1.5

How common is powerlessness among the people you are trying to help? How does powerlessness affect the situations you deal with?

---

## Conclusion

This chapter has explored a number of key elements of the theory base underpinning power. In so doing, it sets the scene for the chapters that follow, particularly Chapter 2 which focuses on the theory base underpinning the related concept of empowerment. It is to be hoped that it has provided a sufficient foundation for you to be able to broaden and deepen your understanding of these important issues. However, you should not make the mistake of assuming that this chapter (or indeed the book as a whole) can provide a sufficient knowledge base in its own right. It is essential that the ideas presented here are seen as stepping stones to further learning, part of a journey of learning, but not the whole journey.

Fook (2002) makes the important point that empowerment involves 'deconstructing' power. In order to promote empowerment, it is therefore very important to have at least a basic understanding of power in all its complexity. Having reviewed the theory base underpinning power, we can now turn our attention to the theoretical underpinnings of empowerment.

## Points to ponder

➤ Consider the three levels of power: personal, cultural and structural. Can you think of an example of each?
➤ How does each of these relate to your work?
➤ Consider each of the four types of power: 'power to'; 'power over'; 'power with' and 'power from within'. How does each of them apply to your area of work?
➤ What dangers do you see in not taking proper account of the workings of power?

# Chapter 2
# Empowerment

Empowerment is a term that is used in different ways by different people. This has been a cause of considerable confusion and has no doubt put many people off. However, it is too important a matter to allow this to continue to happen. My aim in this chapter is therefore to clarify some of the key concepts that underpin empowerment in order to try and remove much of the fog surrounding the subject. Again, it must be noted that space does not permit a full analysis of empowerment theory, and so what is offered is a step in the direction of a fuller understanding of empowerment, rather than the finished product.

## What is empowerment?

In the last decade or so, empowerment has become a buzzword, with all that this entails. Buzzwords often creep into our vocabulary without our necessarily having the opportunity to sit down and examine what they mean, whether or not they are important, how they should be used, and so on.

Empowerment is often defined as 'giving power' to people, but this should not be taken literally. To do so would be to fall into the trap of reductionism, as discussed in Chapter 1. The actual process of empowerment is, as we shall see, far more complex than this.

We should also note that empowering somebody does not necessarily involve giving away one's own power, as such a view is based on a simplistic notion of power that fails to recognise that power can be a good thing (provided that it is not abused or misused). This is a point to which we shall return below.

Empowerment can be defined as helping people gain greater control over their lives and circumstances. It is therefore closely linked to the notion of power. If we relate it to our earlier discussions of power, we can see how it connects with the three levels of power that we identified in Chapter 1:

- *Personal (or psychological)* This includes developing confidence, boosting self-esteem and enhancing skills.
- *Cultural (or discursive)* Cultures often involve frameworks of meaning that can hold people back. For example, certain groups can experience what is known as 'internalised oppression' – that is, they take on board negative 'messages' about themselves as a result of discrimination (Thompson, 2006c). Empowerment at this level can include undermining such frameworks of meaning – for example, by challenging stereotypes.

- *Structural* As we have seen, a person's 'structural location' (his or her place in the network of social divisions) has implications in terms of the distribution of power and opportunities (or 'life chances', to use the technical term). 'Conscientisation' is a form of empowerment that can apply in this regard. It refers to raising people's awareness of how problems experienced often have much to do with wider social and political issues relating to the structure of society (for example, poverty as a structural problem, rather than simply a matter of personal failing).

Given that empowerment relates to these three levels, it is clearly more than just 'enabling' which implies helping people to gain greater control at the psychological level only. Enabling also involves the professional deciding on the goals to be achieved and helping the person concerned to achieve them. Empowerment, by contrast, involves working in partnership and this, in turn, involves negotiating the goals to be achieved together, rather than imposing them. Jack (1995) offers helpful comment:

> The *Concise Oxford Dictionary* defines empowerment as 'authorize, licence (a person to do); give power to; make able (person to do)' – this definition of empowerment has two quite distinct meanings: enablement and empowerment. To authorize, license or make able is a process whereby someone uses their power to enable someone else to do something; what that something is, its nature, goals and extent – is controlled by the enabler. Thus the process of enablement is circumscribed by the power of the enabler and does not involve giving power over that process to the enabled. (p. 11)

Empowerment is not something we can do *to* or *for* people (that is a self-contradictory notion). It is something that we can do only *with* them. As Bounds and Hepburn (1996) put it: 'Individuals cannot be empowered by others, but can be enabled to empower themselves' (p. 15). This has significant implications in terms of recognising that:

- *It is important to develop working in partnership and user involvement* These are both important concepts that will be discussed in more detail in Part Two (working in partnership in Chapter 4; user involvement in Chapter 5). They are based on the recognition that progress is unlikely to be made without the full engagement of the people we are trying to help.
- *It cannot be foisted on people against their will* 'I am going to empower you whether you like it or not' is clearly not a sound foundation for good practice (nor a realistic one). Skills of communication and rapport building are therefore very important.
- *It will sometimes not be possible* While empowerment is clearly an important goal to aim for, we have to be realistic in acknowledging that it will not always be possible to achieve it.

---

**Exercise 2.1**

What skills do you think are involved in working *with* people rather than doing things *to* or *for* them? How widely used are these skills in your area of work? You may find it helpful to compare notes with colleagues on this exercise.

---

We can also see that empowerment can manifest itself within different spheres or domains:

- *The personal/individual* Empowerment can be a matter of individuals being helped in various possible ways to gain greater control over their circumstances.
- *Family, group or team* There is also a collective aspect to empowerment, in the sense that people can help themselves to gain greater control over their circumstances. This is linked to the idea of 'power with', as discussed in Chapter 1.
- *Organisation* Many organisations are 'top down' in their management style and their treatment of staff. Some, however, recognise the value of empowering staff by giving them greater autonomy over their work responsibilities. This encourages creativity rather than simply 'following orders', and can be a significant factor in terms of morale and motivation.
- *Community* It is possible, although often difficult, to help whole communities to gain greater control over their lives and circumstances – for example in relation to involvement in democratic processes.

These different domains show a gradual broadening of scope. The broader the scope, the more far reaching an impact we can potentially have. However, it is also fair to say – and important to note – that the broader the focus we adopt, the more difficult it can be to achieve empowerment. The stakes may be higher, but the chances of success are lower.

---

**Practice Focus 2.1**

Marcia felt nervous on taking up her new post, and was already missing her old team where she had a lot of friends. She was confident, though, that she would settle in soon. However, what she hadn't anticipated was that the culture in her new organisation was so different from her previous one. In her old job she was very closely supervised and often given direct instructions. However, what soon became very clear was that, in her new job, she was expected to work closely with team mates to decide on how to tackle issues rather than simply be told what to do. She found the new approach quite refreshing, if a little daunting at first.

---

Power is not a 'zero sum' concept, in the sense that one person gaining power does not necessarily mean that another person loses power. Empowerment should therefore not be seen simplistically as 'giving away' power. If human services professionals do not have the power to help, their effectiveness is likely to be minimal. The problem is not simply *having* power. Rather, the problem is that such power can be deliberately abused (through corruption, for example) or unwittingly misused (unintentionally discriminating against someone, for example – Thompson, 2003a). Where power is not abused or misused, it can be a positive force to help people solve their problems, achieve their goals and gain greater control over their lives.

Rather than being seen as a 'zero-sum' concept, power is better understood as 'generative': 'empowerment involves the meaningful sharing of power; . . . power is generative and can be created between people' (Deegan, 1997, cited in Linhorst, 2006, p. 4). That is, power can be used to generate more power. This is, in effect, the basis of empowering practice: to use our power not to coerce or to suppress, but rather to help people move towards taking greater control over their lives.

## Theorising empowerment

If we are to take empowerment seriously, then we need to have at least a basic understanding of the theoretical underpinnings of this important concept. It is unfortunately the case that much has been written and spoken about empowerment without adequately considering the theory underlying it. This has contributed a great deal to the oversimplification that we mentioned in Chapter 1. Our task here, therefore, is to explore some of the key issues relating to the theory of empowerment. In such a short introductory book, space will not permit a detailed analysis or a comprehensive treatment of the issues. What is offered, though, should be sufficient to provide a platform for further learning and development; a step in the direction of developing a more sophisticated understanding of the complexities of empowerment.

A key concept in relation to empowerment is that of agency – that is, the ability of individuals (and indeed groups) to make decisions for themselves, to be responsible for their own actions (see the discussion of structuration in Chapter 1). Deterministic theories that deny human agency are based on what is known as 'bad faith' and are characterised by such comments as 'I couldn't help it'. This failure to accept personal responsibility is, of course, not consistent with the notion of empowerment. Empowerment was earlier defined as obtaining greater control over one's life and circumstances. If we deny the basics of human agency and personal responsibility, empowerment becomes a meaningless term. Our first point must therefore be the emphasis on agency as opposed to accepting deterministic theories.

Linked to this is the idea of the 'autotelic self'. This is an idea used by Giddens (1994) to refer to an individual who has:

> an inner confidence which comes from self respect, and one where a sense of ontological security originating in basic trust allows for the positive appreciation of social differences. It refers to a person able to translate potential threats into rewarding challenges. (p. 192)

'Autotelic' derives from the Greek words for 'self' and 'goal' and can therefore be translated as self-directed. This is very relevant to the notion of empowerment, as helping people become more self-directed can be a significant underpinning of some aspects of empowering practice. Helping people have access to sources of power (through advocacy, for example) may be self-defeating if they do not have any sense of personal control or confidence to manage the situation they find themselves in.

---

### Exercise 2.2

How might you be able to help somebody be more 'self-directing'? What strategies might be available to you? What skills would you need to draw on?

---

In order to develop our understanding of empowerment further, it is necessary to challenge a long-standing fallacy, namely, the idea that power is necessarily a bad thing. This negative approach to power can be illustrated in the following passage from Healy (2000):

> This negative approach to power pre-empts inquiry into the local operations of power, as it is necessary only for an individual to be identified as powerful for them to be seen as also an oppressor (Tapper, 1993). This is a significant weakness in terms of developing coalitions with the powerful in so far as there is little opportunity to differentiate between those forms of power that are productive for extending empowerment to participants and those forms that are used to further domination. (p. 111)

As Fook (2002) so aptly puts it: 'Power is both a good and bad thing' (p. 52). To see it simply as domination or oppression is a further example of the oversimplification that has dogged discussions of power and empowerment in some quarters. Power can be used positively or negatively, depending on the circumstances. If we are to understand empowerment (and thereby be in a better position to promote it), we therefore need to move away from such an oversimplified conception and develop a clearer picture of what differentiates the positive use of power from the negative.

As part of this, it is again vitally important to recognise that being powerful cannot automatically be equated with being an oppressor. This is for four reasons:

1. This idea confuses 'power to' with 'power over'. Having 'power to' means that we have a certain potential and this is clearly a good thing. 'Power over', in the sense of domination, however, is a very different entity. Equating being powerful with being an oppressor removes 'power to' from the equation and overemphasises the role of 'power over'.
2. It also disregards the legitimate use of power – that is, the use of authority. There are many circumstances where the operation of power is socially useful, where its absence would be problematic for members of communities (in relation to law and order, for example, or child protection).
3. Nor does it take account of 'power with' or 'power from within'. As we noted in Chapter 1, these are important elements of a theory of power. To equate power with domination and thus oppression is to present one part of the whole as if it represented the full picture.
4. It makes the idea of empowerment nonsensical. If being powerful is to be equated with being an oppressor, why would we want to play a part in empowering people? We would then only be making people who are now relatively powerless into future oppressors. This clearly illustrates the theoretical inadequacy of this long-standing, but misguided assumption that having power and being oppressive are necessarily the same thing.

The problems inherent in such a reductionist approach are illustrated well in Healy's (2000) comments as follows:

> Denzin (quoted in Fine, 1994, p. 79) notes that critical approaches to the study of power tend to:
>> create self (colonizer) and other (colonized) as dichotomous categories, oppositions defined out of clearly defined cultural, ethnic, racial and gendered differences. Such treatments (after Derrida and Bakhtin) fail to treat the complexities and contradictions that define membership in each category (p. 79).
> (pp. 69–70)

The problem, then, is not power *per se*; the problem arises as a result of the misuse or abuse of power, a point to which we shall return below.

Another key term is that of resilience. This refers to the ability to become stronger through adversity, to be able to 'bounce back' in the wake of situations that could be harmful to us. For example, illness may make someone weaker, whereas being able to cope with the illness may make that person stronger (in terms of 'power from within', for example). We have to make sure that we are not failing to do justice to people's strengths when we assume that certain circumstances will leave them weaker.

This is linked with what is often referred to these days as a strengths perspective. This involves moving away from a deficit model in which people who are receiving help from professionals are in some way seen as inadequate, as Moss (2005) so clearly illustrates:

We (the professional workers) are strong, capable, insightful, well-trained, resourceful, able to solve problems, and to be successful helpers. You (the service user/client), by contrast, are weak, unable to solve your problems, lacking insight, somewhat helpless, and therefore so fortunate to have us to work with you to give you the benefit of our skills and knowledge, so that some measure of improvement can be achieved in your mediocre lives. (p. 74)

---

### Exercise 2.3

How can you make sure you do not fall into the trap illustrated in Moss's comments above? How can you ensure that you avoid such a patronising and potentially destructive approach?

---

### Practice Focus 2.2

Marcia soon became aware of other differences between her new employing organisation and her previous one. In particular, she realised that her new colleagues placed a lot of emphasis on identifying, and helping to build on, people's strengths. This was something she wasn't used to and it made her realise how, in her previous job, she had wasted so much positive potential by concentrating too narrowly on the problems and negatives of the situations she was dealing with. It made her determined to make sure she didn't make the same mistake in her new post.

---

We can see that empowerment is a means of helping people identify and build on strengths. Often people do not need help in doing this; they are perfectly capable of doing so unaided. However, there are many circumstances in which people may need help in this regard. This includes the following:

- *Fear* Jack (1995) refers to a study by Ellis (1992) which shows that fear can be a very significant factor.
- *Low self-esteem* A lack of confidence and negative self-image can arise in certain circumstances, and this can lead to a vicious circle in which a person's ability to cope is undermined, leading to a further drop in low self-esteem. This can often manifest itself in what I referred to earlier as 'internalised oppression'. This refers to situations where someone is a member of an oppressed group and internalises the negative images of, and assumptions about, that group. For example, as a result of ageism older people often internalise negative images of themselves. However, note that I said *often*. It would be a serious oversimplification to assume that this is always the case. That assumption would undermine the notion of resilience.
- *Pressure from others* For example, if somebody is being abused, then this may undermine their coping abilities at that particular time, and thus their ability to a) deal with the situation, and b) learn from it.

- *Anxiety* We are often dealing with situations that involve high levels of anxiety. This can stand in the way of the use of people's strengths. It can act as a barrier. Part of the professional role may therefore be to help deal with high levels of anxiety in order to enable people to be able to build on their strengths.
- *Conflict* Situations involving conflict can sometimes bring out the best in people but may also have the effect of, as with anxiety, acting as a barrier to being able to draw on one's strengths.
- *Pain* If somebody is in pain as a result of illness or injury, this may also prevent that person from drawing on their strengths.
- *Grief* Experiencing a major loss can have significant consequences in terms of our coping ability.
- *Debt* In Chapter 14, we shall look at the significance of poverty in relation to empowerment. Debt can be a major problem that can lead to a vicious circle, in so far as the pressures of being in debt can stand in the way of people being able to make use of their personal resources to address their problems.
- *Mental health problems* It is sometimes the case that people who are experiencing mental health problems are unable to draw on their own abilities or personal resources.
- *Learning disabilities* Here too, the problems involved in some forms of learning disability can lead to strengths not being realised.
- *Alcohol or drug misuse* The effects of relying on such substances can be very detrimental in terms of being able to tackle the underlying issues.

The key part of the strengths approach is the use of narratives. A narrative, literally, is a story. In order to help people develop and build on their resilience, we can use the technique of helping people look at meanings they attach to certain aspects of their lives (the narrative or story around these issues) and see whether helpful changes can be made to this. Parton and O'Byrne (2000, p. 50) cast light on this as follows:

> Storytelling produces and reforms the family 'by legitimising means and power relations that privilege parents over children, men over women, and middle class over lower class'. But just as the story telling 'participates in social control of the family' it can also 'foster resistance and tactics that contest dominant meanings and power relations'. (Langellier and Peterson, 1993, p. 50)

Also, in drawing on the work of de Shazer (1985), a well-known exponent of narrative-based work, Parton and O'Byrne comment that:

> De Shazer says that our expertise needs to shift, from being providers of solutions and meanings, to expert conversationalists who can help people to demolish the old destructive stories that oppress and disempower them *by moving towards a co-authored new story.* (p. 59)

What this involves, then, is helping people develop less oppressive or less self-defeating narratives. It enables them to look at their life and circumstances from a different angle. This can be extremely important, as experiences of abuse, discrimination and oppression often have the effect of leaving people with a distorted understanding of their situation, frequently a very negative, self-defeating understanding of that situation.

---

### Practice Focus 2.3

Marcia started to realise that, by focusing more on people's strengths, she was increasingly coming across examples of low self-esteem. So many of the people she was trying to help seemed to have had life experiences that had left them with low expectations of themselves and what they could achieve in life. It dawned on her that she would need to look at ways in which she could get round this, as it was such a significant obstacle to progress for so many people. When her supervisor told her about the narrative approach and what it entailed, she was delighted to find such a potentially helpful approach and she looked forward to finding out more about it and putting it into practice.

---

The concept of 'voice' is also central to an understanding of empowerment. By voice we mean the ability of people (especially disadvantaged people whose wishes are often disregarded) to make their wishes and feelings known, to have a say in what happens to them. This can manifest itself in terms of user involvement, to be discussed in Chapter 5, and also in relation to partnership which is the subject matter of Chapter 4. Voice is vitally important because, without voice, we are simply paying lip service to the notion of empowerment. Working with people in an empowering way must therefore involve listening carefully, doing what we reasonably can to give voice to the concerns and wishes of those people we are trying to help.

An example of this is what is known as the 'exchange' approach to interviewing and assessment:

> The exchange model of assessment features in the work of Smale et al. (1993). This model is contrasted with the questioning and procedural models. The three models can be described in the following terms:
> - *Questioning* This model is based on the idea that the worker is an expert in people and their problems and needs. The assessment, based on this expertise, involves identifying need and deciding the best way to meet that need. This is very similar to the elitist model of assessment in which the worker is the expert who 'knows best'.
> - *Procedural* This type of assessment involves gathering information to establish whether the client meets identified eligibility criteria. It is primarily a means of rationing scarce resources.

- *Exchange* This model is one based on partnership, in so far as it involves the worker facilitating the process by which client and worker jointly identify needs and explore ways of meeting such needs. . . .

The exchange model is clearly the best suited of the three when it comes to working in partnership. Using this model means that responsibility for the situation is neither wrested from clients nor dumped upon them. Rather, it is shared . . . (Thompson and Thompson, 2005, pp. 60–61)

This model was developed in relation to community care, but it can easily be adapted to apply across the human services and indeed in a management context. It is just one example of how professional practice can be geared towards promoting voice for people who traditionally have little or no say in how matters develop in relation to services they receive or help that they are offered.

---

### Exercise 2.4

What degree of 'voice' do the people you are seeking to help typically have? In what ways can you work towards increasing the amount, range and effectiveness of such voice?

---

The importance of crisis is also a further feature of empowerment theory. A crisis is a turning point in somebody's life. It is the point at which the situation can get significantly better or significantly worse. (If it is likely to continue without getting significantly better or significantly worse, then by definition it is not a crisis.) Crisis intervention is a long-standing professional approach to these issues which focuses on maximising the positive potential of the crisis. It involves making the best use of the opportunities for growth and learning that are presented within the crisis situation. This is to be contrasted with 'crisis survival' which is geared simply towards helping people get through a stormy period in their lives. Crisis intervention can be very empowering in so far as it can enable people to grow and learn from their experience while crisis survival is more likely to lead to dependency creation. The skills involved in crisis intervention are therefore vitally important skills when it comes to empowering practice.

Also in crisis situations, it is important to make sure that we do not abuse the power we have. This is because when people are in crisis, they are very susceptible to influence from others. For example, if somebody is feeling desperate and all at sea, then he or she is much more likely to respond to advice and guidance from another person than would normally be the case. The potential for abusing power over people in vulnerable circumstances as a result of crisis is therefore quite considerable. We therefore have to make sure that we are not drawn into this form of abuse of power by the pressures of the crisis situation.

Crisis can also be linked with resilience because what crisis intervention is geared towards is helping to make use of resilience and, where possible, develop it further – by helping people to gain whatever positive benefits they can from what may be in other respects very problematic circumstances.

One further point worth emphasising in relation to theory of empowerment is the importance of endings. It is surprising that so much literature on professional practice in the human services neglects the question of endings. There are many examples of texts that discuss processes of, for example, assessment, intervention, review and evaluation but say little or nothing in terms of how best to bring one's involvement to a close. Endings can be seen as opportunities to affirm and congratulate, to celebrate success and note progress made. If endings are not handled appropriately, they can undermine and create dependency – that is, if somebody has made good progress through the help of another person, but the success involved is not acknowledged in an ending, then when that person needs help in future, they are likely to go back to the person they asked the help from in the first place rather than draw on the learning from the experience that they have had. This is a classic example of how not to do empowering work as the creation of dependency is the antithesis of empowerment. It needs to be remembered that avoiding dependency is a primary feature of empowerment work and endings have an important part to play in that.

## Conclusion

This chapter has explored the complex issues of what is empowerment and how do we make sense of it. Of necessity, it has not been comprehensive but it should, none the less, be a useful contribution to developing our understanding. This chapter concludes Part One of the book, with its focus on power and empowerment theory. This now sets the scene for Part Two where we shall explore the implications of power and empowerment for professional practice and management.

It is perhaps apt to conclude Part One with the following important comment from Donelan (1995) which succeeds in getting to the heart of the matter: 'For all its complexity, empowerment is a simple cry for a more egalitarian, democratic, and humanitarian social order' (p. 44).

## Points to ponder

➤ How realistic do you feel empowering practice is in your area of work?
➤ What obstacles stand in the way of progress?
➤ What steps can you take to give empowerment a higher profile?
➤ Whose support can you draw upon to try and rise to these challenges?

# Part Two: Power and Empowerment in Practice

## Introduction

---

Chapters 1 and 2 have shown just how complex a field of study we engage with when we seek to make sense of power and empowerment. We need to bear this complexity in mind when we try to link the theory to practice. This is because, as was noted earlier, practice in relation to empowerment has tended to be characterised by oversimplification. Good practice needs to be based on a more sophisticated understanding of power and empowerment. Part Two therefore presents quite a challenge: trying to make a reality of empowering practice without falling foul of an unduly simplistic approach to the subject.

Part Two is divided into five chapters. The first of these, Chapter 3, is concerned with 'self-empowerment'. It is based on the idea that staff and managers will find it difficult to play a part in promoting empowerment if they are not themselves empowered – that is, they are not in control of their own workloads and duties. This is an important issue, as organisations that disempower their staff are also, indirectly, disempowering the people they are trying to serve.

Chapter 4 is entitled *Working in Partnership* and explores what is involved in effective collaboration between staff and their clientele. It considers the skills involved as well as other key issues, including the limitations of partnership working. Chapter 5 builds on Chapter 4 by addressing the related topic of 'user involvement'. It examines what is involved in making sure that, as far as possible, the people we are seeking to help are actively involved in the process rather than passive recipients of help. This raises a number of important issues, some of which fly in the face of traditional approaches to professional practice with their 'top-down' emphasis.

Chapter 6 follows on from this challenge to traditional professionalism by outlining an alternative model of professionalism that is more consistent with forms of practice based on empowerment. Chapter 7 is entitled *Making Empowerment Real*. It explores the steps that need to be taken to make sure that a commitment to empowerment is more than rhetorical, that it has its roots in reality.

# Chapter 3
# Self-empowerment

'How am I supposed to help empower people when I feel totally taken for granted and used by our managers, who seem to have no understanding of the pressures of my job and who are only content if I tick boxes and help them meet precious bloody targets?' Comment from a course participant as part of a discussion on empowerment.

Clearly, a very important point to note is that, if professional staff in the human services feel that they are not empowered – that is, that they are not in control of their work, that they are simply following orders or ticking boxes – they will struggle to play a positive role in helping to empower others. Eastman (1995) echoes the same theme when he argues that:

> If I am devalued by my managers how can I sustain my regard of the client or carer's rights to be at the very centre of my practice? Staff and managers who feel under siege cannot, in my view, sustain an approach to users that focuses on high quality responses or 'humane standards' in service provision. Staff who are disempowered by silence, brevity, snubbery, insults, blaming, discrediting, yelling and screaming from managers exist in an organizational culture of corruption which inevitably leads to dysfunction and further discounting and disempowerment of the service user. (pp. 261–2)

From this we can see that it is therefore vitally important that professional staff are treated with dignity, as valued professionals, with the appropriate level of respect and autonomy. This is a point to which we shall return below when we discuss professionalism in more detail (see Chapter 6). For present purposes, it is important to note that helping to empower others involves:

- *the use of a professional knowledge base* It is intricate and challenging work that goes far beyond 'common sense' understanding of people and their problems;
- *the use of support networks* The demands of practice are such that it is unrealistic to expect staff to do well without proper channels of support; and
- *taking the opportunity to challenge or remove barriers* Simply following standard procedures or adopting routine practices will not get us very far. We need to draw on the critical thinking involved in reflective practice by identifying and tackling obstacles to progress.

None of this is possible if we adopt a narrow, mechanistic view of the role of human services workers and indeed of managers. If we are committed to empowerment, then we need to do everything we reasonably can (individually and collectively) to make sure that workplaces are supportive of staff and their professionalism – and to challenge accordingly where they are not.

A key theme of this book is that empowerment is not something we do *to* people. From this we can see, then, that all empowerment is a form of self-empowerment. What we are doing in developing empowering practice is trying to help people empower themselves. As Simon (1990) puts it:

> The one function that . . . anyone else *cannot* perform for another person is that of empowerment. Empowerment is a reflexive activity, a process capable of being initiated and sustained only by the agent or subject who seeks power or self-determination. (p. 32, cited in Linhorst, 2005, p. 9)

However, in this chapter, we focus on the (self-)empowerment of professional staff and managers. This is because staff and managers who are disempowered are in a weak position to support others in their attempts to empower themselves. It is therefore important to explore how staff and managers can focus on their own empowerment (and indeed support each other in doing so). If these issues are not taken seriously, there can be detrimental consequences for all concerned:

- *staff* Stress and burnout can arise in highly pressurised circumstances where people feel they have little or no control;
- *managers* Managers, too, are not immune to stress and burnout, but there is also the issue that their work becomes even more difficult, if not impossible, if they are relying on disempowered staff;
- *the people we are seeking to help* We are highly unlikely to achieve effective, high-quality practice in a context of disempowerment, and so the people we serve also lose out; and
- *the employing organisation* An organisation characterised by, or with pockets of, a culture of disempowerment is highly unlikely to be a successful organisation.

We shall examine each of these areas in turn.

## Staff

Stress has been recognised as a significant problem in modern workplaces. If staff are to do the best job they can, then they need to be protected from the harmful effects of stress. A key factor in this regard is *control*, as it is a very significant issue in relation to stress. See, for example, the discussion of the 'locus of control' in Thompson *et al.* (1994). People can generally cope with significant levels of pressure provided that they are in control. It is when we feel that we are losing control (or have already lost it) that we can start to experience uncomfortable levels of stress. Low levels of control have been recognised to contribute to low levels of morale within the workplace. For example, the Health and Safety Executive include 'control' as one of the management standards they have adopted in their efforts to combat workplace stress (www.hse.gov.uk/stress/standards/index.htm). Lacking control can also lead to defeatism, cynicism and 'learned helplessness' (Seligman, 1975). This, in turn, can lead to burnout and demoralisation. Burnt out or demoralised staff will not be in a good position to exercise the necessary skills and demonstrate the sensitivity required to make a positive contribution to empowering practice. The link between control as a factor in the workplace and empowerment is therefore a significant one, as both relate to power.

In circumstances where people are stressed, burnt out and/or demoralised, values can be abandoned. In desperate times, people – even kind-hearted committed people – can leave their values behind and can take short cuts. This can have the result of returning to more traditional modes of practice that are associated with dependency creation and paternalistic models of practice, rather than making a contribution towards empowerment.

---

**Practice Focus 3.1**

Gavin was a very committed worker who took pride in doing a good job. However, when his department was severely short of staff, he felt the need to cut corners just to get through the day. He found himself getting into a whirl of activity, not entirely sure what he was doing. He felt very uncomfortable about the very superficial way he was doing his job and the poor service he was giving people who needed his help, but he could see no other way of coping. It was only after this period was over that he realised that he had allowed himself too easily to compromise his values. This made him determined to look for other ways of dealing with the pressures if that situation should arise again.

---

Stress and a feeling of a lack of control can also lead to self-disempowerment – that is, staff may experience low levels of confidence or professional low self-esteem which can result in low expectations. These, in turn, can result in low levels of achievement. In this way a vicious circle can so easily arise: low levels of confidence – low expectations – low levels of achievement – low confidence reinforced, and so on. It is therefore important that we do not allow issues like stress, burnout and low levels of morale to continue to be significant factors in the workplace, as these are detrimental towards any attempt to promote empowering forms of practice.

A major danger in the human services is the development of a bureaucratic or mechanistic approach. Often this is the result of burnout, as mentioned above. People can feel so overloaded, including at an emotional level, that they may adopt what they perceive as a safer approach of not getting involved, of simply going through the motions. This can lead to significant deskilling and a blunting of critical faculties. That is, people who get drawn into bureaucratic or mechanistic approaches fail to draw on the skills they have and, indeed, to develop those skills further. They are also more likely to fail to deal with issues critically, to apply their powers of reason and analysis and look below the surface of the circumstances they are dealing with. They are also less likely to learn from their experience, making continuous professional development an empty phrase. Clearly, this is not a recipe for good practice and is certainly not a foundation for empowering practice. This is a point to which we shall return in Chapter 6 in relation to professionalism.

We noted earlier that a vicious circle of low expectations can easily arise. However, a related vicious circle of disempowerment can occur: if staff feel that they are disempowered, that they are unduly hampered by bureaucracy, unthinking mechanistic approaches, unrealistic workloads, and so on, then they are going to be ill-equipped to play a key role in helping to empower others. This vicious circle needs to be contrasted with a virtuous circle of empowerment where staff have perhaps very heavy, but none the less realistic, workloads where their skills are being used and developed, where they are being valued and appreciated for the hard work they do, often in very difficult circumstances. This latter scenario can bring out the best in them which, in turn, means that they will be much better equipped to demonstrate the skills and sensitivity needed to act in a way that promotes empowerment.

## Managers

The role of managers is a pivotal one, in so far as managers have a significant part to play in supporting their staff in the direction of empowerment, but managers, particularly in terms of their leadership responsibilities, are also significant players in terms of shaping a culture of empowerment – for example, in challenging bureaucratic and mechanistic approaches that demoralise staff. Through this, managers have a key role in shaping good practice, but they also have a role in terms of contributing to the overall culture of the organisation – in other words, promoting empowerment, not just downwards through the official hierarchy, but upwards and across the organisation as part of an attempt to develop and sustain a culture of empowering practice.

A long-standing approach to management theory is that of theories X and Y (McGregor, 1987). Theory X is based on the idea that employees are unlikely to be motivated and give of their best unless they are closely monitored and heavily controlled. Theory Y, by contrast, is based on the notion that employees will be keen to make a contribution to their workplace because it is in their interests to have an enjoyable work experience. This approach has further been developed by the introduction of Theory Z (Ouchi, 1981) which argues that: 'If individuals can identify closely with the organisation as a whole, then organisational performance will be intrinsically rewarding to the individual' (Mullins, 1996, p. 549).

These theoretical approaches bring us back to the important role of leadership. A leader is someone who is able to clarify the goals that staff are working towards and inspire them in that direction. Leaders pull rather than push, in the sense that a good leader will not need to try and force staff to undertake certain duties, they will have created a culture in which staff are keen to undertake those duties – for example, in relation to promoting empowerment.

A key factor in terms of empowerment for managers is the importance of supervision. Supervision is a process through which workload is not only monitored in a technical way, but in which staff are given the support they need to carry out their duties to the best of their abilities and to learn from their experiences in the process. Supervision, when undertaken appropriately and skilfully, can be very empowering. When it is reduced to simply checking up on whether staff have carried out their duties or not, it can be very disheartening, demoralising and, thus, disempowering. It is therefore important for managers to take seriously the challenge of supervision and to develop the necessary skills if they are to play a significant part in promoting a culture of empowerment.

---

### Practice Focus 3.2

Kim was finding her work very difficult. She was committed to empowerment, but at every turn she encountered discouragements: a lack of co-operation here, a setback there. She was beginning to feel very downhearted. However, when she had supervision with Laeka, she felt as though she had had her batteries recharged. Laeka's skilful use of supervision gave her a new lease of energy and commitment. Kim started to realise that supervision could be empowering if carried out skilfully and she was grateful Laeka had those skills.

---

Finally, in relation to managers, it should be noted that empowerment is more than delegation. Reference has already been made to the strong tendency to oversimplify issues relating to power and empowerment. A clear example of this oversimplification is the widespread tendency for empowerment in the workplace to be seen as little more than delegation. Instead of a manager deciding what needs doing and supporting staff in doing that, he or she gives the overall task to staff for them to take responsibility for. While empowerment in this managerial sense can be seen to involve an element of delegation, to see it as nothing but delegation is a gross oversimplification and a dangerous one at that, because it means that a very positive process, which is what empowerment can and should be, actually becomes a negative process which leads to feelings of resentment, alienation and potentially low morale.

## Client/patient/service user

A central theme of empowerment is the need to avoid dependency, but a disempowered, demoralised worker may gain some (inappropriate and ultimately destructive) sense of satisfaction from having someone becoming dependent on them. In this way, disempowerment can breed disempowerment. The significance of staff being adequately supported and valued cannot therefore be overemphasised. This is because organisations that pay lip service to empowerment and do not think through the implications of an ethos of empowerment for staff and managers, will do a significant disservice to the people they are seeking to help.

A final point worthy of note is that empowerment should not be seen as 'giving away' power (as noted in Chapter 1). From the arguments I have put forward in this chapter, it should be clear that it is not a matter of power being a fixed sum and therefore the more power a client/patient/service user has, the less power a worker is to have. We must be careful, therefore, not to fall into the common trap of oversimplifying empowerment by assuming that it involves some notion of giving away power in a simplistic sense.

Empowered managers supporting empowered practitioners is a much stronger basis for supporting the empowerment of the people we serve than the alternative of a stressed and demoralised group of people struggling against the odds to provide high-quality services.

## The employing organisation

As we have noted, managers and practitioners who feel they have little or no power or control over the work that they are doing are likely to feel stressed and demoralised. That has implications for not only the people we are trying to help, for managers and staff, but also for the organisation as a whole. Organisations where people have little or no autonomy and thus no sense of control or direction are likely to be harder to manage (see my comments about Theories X and Y above). They may also suffer in terms of:

- *Recruitment and retention* Staff are less likely to stay in such an organisation, and potential new staff are unlikely to be attracted by the prospect of working in such an atmosphere.
- *Workforce development* Learning and development will be significantly hampered by working in such a disempowered and disempowering setting.
- *Morale and motivation* This all adds up to low levels of morale and motivation, and thus to lower quality and quantity of work.

Clearly, then, a commitment to an informed approach to empowerment has much to offer all concerned.

## Points to ponder

➤ How much control and autonomy do you have over your work?
➤ If it is a great deal, how can you use this to help empower others?
➤ If it is a little, how can you seek to extend it?
➤ Who can you collaborate with to promote a greater emphasis on empowerment?

# Chapter 4
# Working in partnership

An important theme that emerged in Part One is that a central part of empowerment is working in partnership – that is, working *with* people rather than doing things *to* or *for* them. As Rowlands (1998) so aptly puts it:

> We need to move away from any notion of empowerment . . . as something that can be done 'to' people or 'for' people. Empowerment is important not as an instrumentalist notion or rhetorical device, but it is an active tool which, if used thoughtfully, can be used to achieve change with justice. (p. 30)

We therefore need to take seriously the importance of developing and consolidating a partnership-based approach to our work. We shall see in Chapter 6 that traditional approaches to practice based on notions of the professional as the dominant person are incompatible with empowerment and can therefore no longer be sustained. Approaches based on partnership – that is, involving people in decision making and so on as far as possible, rather than making decisions for them – are far more of a sound foundation for practice (and, indeed, for management).

## Developing partnership

Developing partnership can be seen to raise a number of key issues, not least the following:

- *Communication and rapport building* This is an essential part of working in partnership. We must have highly developed communication skills and the ability to 'engage' with people – that is, to form a rapport (such skills are often referred to as 'engagement skills'). There is an important distinction to be drawn between a relationship and a rapport. A relationship may take a long time to build up, and often human services professionals do not have the relative luxury of that amount of time to develop a positive relationship. However, a *rapport* is something that can be established very quickly if the professional concerned has the appropriate skills and abilities. A key part of this is the ability to listen effectively, to be open to hearing what is being said, rather than simply wanting to establish our own agenda and our own way forward.
- *Clarity about goals* It is extremely important that we are clear about what are the desired outcomes and means of achieving them. This is a process of joint

agenda setting. It would be a return to the sad old days of elitist professionalism (see Chapter 6) for the professional staff member to make unilateral decisions about where our intervention should be taking us and how we are going to get there. Working in partnership as part of a broader agenda of empowerment involves jointly establishing what we are trying to achieve and jointly establishing how we are going to achieve it. This joint approach can have the effect of increasing motivation and decreasing resistance.

- *Managing conflict constructively* Many people regard conflict as the breakdown of normal interpersonal relations. However, a more realistic perspective recognises that conflict is part and parcel of everyday interpersonal relations. It would be naïve to think that working in partnership implies not having any conflict. A more realistic perspective on this involves acknowledging that effective partnership work entails having the skills and commitment necessary to manage conflict constructively and appropriately. This is partly a matter of assertiveness and negotiation skills, but there are also specific issues relating to conflict management – we shall return to this point below.

---

**Practice Focus 4.1**

Nira spent a considerable part of her career being afraid of entering into conflict. She saw her job as being about helping people and regarded conflict as what happens when you fail to maintain a good working relationship. However, after attending a course on conflict management, she began to appreciate that conflict is actually a normal part of everyday life (for example, people having conflicting aims or wishes). It became apparent to her also that managing conflict constructively can be far more effective than simply trying to avoid it. She decided that she would adopt a different approach to conflict in future, as she now realised that handling conflict skilfully is an important part of empowerment.

---

The term 'partnership' derives from the word *part*ner and this implies that everybody involved plays a part. The essence of partnership, as we have already noted, is working with people, not doing things to or for them – in other words, working in collaboration on as equal a footing as we can possibly establish. There are two main types of partnership: that between worker and client and that between worker and other workers, whether within their own agency or other parts of the multidisciplinary network. In this chapter we are going to focus on the first of these because the idea of developing worker-client partnerships is an important underpinning of empowering practice. This is not to say that the second type is not important. Indeed, multidisciplinary power battles at the expense of our clientele can be a significant problem. However, my focus here is on how partnership can form the basis of helping to promote empowerment among the people we serve.

This chapter should provide a platform for developing an understanding of user involvement which we shall address in Chapter 5. User involvement is premised on the notion of partnership for without some notion of working in partnership, user involvement is fairly meaningless.

A basic part of working in partnership is recognising the difference between what is meant by partnership as opposed to paternalism. Partnership is based on 'power with', whereas paternalism is based on the idea of 'power over'. 'Power with' can be very helpful in developing the potential for 'power from within' as well as 'power to'.

There is a lot of material to be found now about working in partnership. This illustrates how much we have recognised the importance of this aspect of professional practice in recent years. We have also begun to recognise how many skills are involved in working in partnership. These include the following:

- *Communication and rapport building* As mentioned earlier, it is important to be able to communicate effectively both verbally and in writing if we are to be able to work in partnership. However, effective partnership working goes beyond simple communication. There is also the important matter of rapport building – what I referred to earlier as 'engagement'. Rapport building comprises largely of communication skills, but it is possible to be able to communicate very well at a technical level, but still not have the ability to form a rapport with the person or persons we are engaged with (or should be engaged with). There are therefore significant challenges involved in developing the advanced-level communication and engagement skills that form the foundation of high-quality partnership working.
- *Negotiation* There will inevitably be situations where it is necessary to negotiate with the people we are working with. It would be naïve to assume that everything will fall neatly into place. The skills of negotiation are closely allied to those of assertiveness. This means that we do not bully others into doing what we want them to do, but nor do we allow others to push us into doing things that we feel are inappropriate. The skills of negotiation are therefore essential building blocks of working in partnership. Efforts devoted to developing these are likely to be well rewarded in terms of improved outcomes.
- *Conflict management* This is closely related to the point about negotiation. Conflict is an ever-present aspect of social and professional life, in the sense that conflicts of interest, perspective and direction are basic parts of human existence. We have to recognise that there will be times when we will be in conflict, and where basic negotiation skills are not sufficient. Experience and, where available, training in these issues should be an important part of developing the necessary conflict management skills.

- *Empathy* There has been much discussion about emotional intelligence in recent years. A key part of this is the ability to recognise other people's emotions and this is basically what empathy is about. It is not necessary for us to share the emotions of the people we are trying to help (that could be very destructive for us), but we do have to have the sensitivity to recognise people's feelings and respond appropriately.
- *Self-management* We have to be able to deal with our own anxieties and needs. This involves avoiding situations arising in which such anxieties or personal issues lead us to duck out of demanding aspects of the situation or, at the opposite extreme, to take over and thus dominate.
- *Risk management* In working with others, we have to recognise that there will be times when risks have to be taken into consideration. In some forms of work, this is a daily occurrence, but in all forms of people work, there will be at least an element of this from time to time. Empowerment does not mean leaving people to cope with their risks unsupported as if dumping responsibility on them. In professional settings, risk management is generally a shared responsibility, and so it is important that we take this seriously and, over time, develop the skills necessary.

It is also very important to recognise that partnership involves being open to learning. Different people will have different perspectives, and it would be arrogant and unhelpful for us to assume that 'we know best'. It is helpful for us to be more open to what other people's experiences and views can bring to the situation. This is a point to which we shall return in Chapter 6 when we discuss professionalism. That discussion will be concerned with trying to find the balance between the two unhelpful extremes of (1) 'we know best' and (2) simply following instructions, with little or no confidence in our professional abilities. The first is an example of paternalism and is not something we would wish to promote. The second involves bypassing professional expertise and in situations where people are in need or distressed, there will be circumstances where they are likely to act in a way that they will regret. Simply following instructions will not therefore be helpful in this regard. We may sometimes have to challenge (gently, constructively and supportively) what the people we are trying to help are doing, if it is harmful to themselves or to others. The emphasis is on working together in order to maximise positive outcomes, and this involves avoiding those unhelpful extremes of paternalism on the one hand and neglecting our professional duties by simply following instructions on the other.

---

### Practice Focus 4.2

Mari had been very hurt when a complaint was made against her. She worked very hard and was very committed to doing a good job. It was therefore a very painful experience to be interviewed by a complaints investigator. However, it came as a significant relief to be exonerated as a result of the investigation. She had disagreed with a family about the wisdom of a course of action they were proposing, as she felt it would be unwise, counterproductive and quite possibly harmful. When she discovered that they had complained about her comments about this course of action, she began to wonder whether she had overstepped the mark. It therefore came as very good news when the investigator's report commented that not only was her disagreement with the family quite justified, but also that it would have been a dereliction of her professional duties if she had not raised her concerns about what they were planning to do.

## Limits to partnership working

There are, of course, limits to partnership working. There will be times, for example, when people are not willing or not ready to work in partnership (perhaps due to a lack of trust as a result of previous negative experiences at the hands of disempowering professionals). There may be other situations where people are unable to work in partnership because of, for example, the severity of a mental health problem, learning disability, or medical condition such as dementia.

However, not working in partnership runs the risk of alienating people (generating mistrust and resentment – or adding to existing mistrust and resentment), and so abandoning partnership should therefore be a last resort. It is extremely important that we should not allow the limits to partnership to be overemphasised, leading to a distorted situation in which the potential for partnership is overshadowed by concerns about obstacles to effective partnership working. The efforts involved in working in partnership can often be considerable, but it is generally worth the effort to do so in terms of improved working relations and the potential for more positive outcomes.

## Theory and practice

I have written elsewhere about the problems that can arise when a wedge is driven between theory and practice (Thompson, 2000). This applies very clearly to both partnership and empowerment. Both are areas that can easily be accepted at a rhetorical level, but which are not necessarily translated into practice. This is illustrated in the following comment from Servian (1996) who is describing the findings from a research study:

> There were also differences between empowering theory and disempowering practice. Managers and other players saw the development of user and carer participation as empowering, but all players also saw the actual process of participation as disempowering through incomprehensible agendas and unwelcoming membership. (p. 36)

Having a theory of empowerment through partnership working is a good start, but what is also needed is the ability to relate the theory to practice. This is partly a matter of reflective practice (making sure that we are thinking critically about our practice and drawing on our professional knowledge base, rather than relying on habit, routine or guesswork) and partly good management – for example, through the use of supervision to make sure that practice is consistent with the underlying knowledge and value base.

## Conclusion

Working in partnership is not an easy option, but it is none the less a vitally important option. We have to make sure that workload pressures or other distractions do not get in the way of making a proper commitment to promoting empowerment through working together.

In some ways, partnership working goes against the grain of traditional models of professionalism based on the idea of using professional expertise in a unilateral way towards a passive recipient of help. Developing partnership is therefore closely linked to the development of new forms of professionalism, and that will be the subject matter of Chapter 6. However, before we explore those issues, we also need to examine another topic closely linked with partnership, namely user involvement. It is to this important topic that we now turn.

## Points to ponder

➤ How well equipped do you feel in terms of the skills required for working in partnership?
➤ What areas of strength can you build on and what areas for development can you build up?
➤ What obstacles to partnership working can you identify?
➤ What can you do about them (individually and collectively)?

# Chapter 5
# User involvement

User involvement can be seen as an extension of the notion of partnership, in so far as it is based on the important basis that: (i) positive outcomes are more likely where people are actively involved in the issues that affect them; and (ii) it is unethical to exclude people from such matters. However, it is worth exploring as a topic in its own right because it has significant implications that go beyond established notions of working in partnership.

## Citizenship

A particularly important concept here is that of 'citizenship'. Lewis (2004a), in referring to the work of Frazer and Gordon (1994), comments that social citizenship:

- locates us in a relationship to the state whereby we can make *legitimate* claims;
- locates us in an institutional infrastructure through which we are *connected* to others – that is, to those with whom we share citizenship;
- accords to us a *status* from which we can gain a sense of self-worth and dignity;
- provides a conduit to *resources* – that is, to welfare services and benefits. (p. 3)

This short, but very significant passage illustrates the relevance of citizenship in relation to user involvement. Users of services have rights ('can make *legitimate* claims'); can help each other and learn from each other (are *connected* to others); are entitled to self-worth and dignity; and have access to resources. User involvement can be seen as part of a commitment to citizenship as a professional value.

## How can service users be involved?

User involvement involves a number of elements. The key ones can be identified as:

- *Case by case* This is very much at the heart of partnership. As a professional works on a particular case, he or she needs to be making sure that the people we are trying to help are actively involved in the process, that it is not something that is happening *to* them, but something that they are playing an active role in developing. Change that is imposed on people is rarely, if ever, as effective as change that is actively embraced by the people affected by it. This is connected with the notion of authenticity, as discussed in Chapter 1 – that is, it is important to recognise the role of personal autonomy. We are dealing with human beings who can and should make their own decisions, not puppets to act at the bidding of more powerful individuals or organisations.

- *Policy development and evaluation* What happens on a case-by-case basis will owe a great deal to the policies that the particular professional or professionals involved are pursuing. In order to get a true sense of partnership and involvement, it is therefore important for clients to play a part in contributing to the policy development process and, indeed, of evaluating policies to ensure that they are achieving what they set out to do. We have to recognise, though, that pressures of work can easily lead us into focusing on professional issues and losing sight of the service user perspective – especially in settings where staff are not themselves empowered (see Chapter 3). If service users are not involved, we run the risk of developing policies and services that are out of touch with people's needs.

- *Education and training* To establish fully the importance of user involvement, it is important to have clients involved in the development and delivery of education and training. There have been some tokenistic attempts to do this that have largely failed (largely because insufficient effort was made to clarify roles and establish clearly how service user involvement could be of benefit – simply inviting one or more service users to attend a training course is not enough on its own). However, on the positive side, there are also examples to be found of positive working practices where recipients of help from human services professionals have had a meaningful role in contributing to learning and development for the professionals involved.

- *Research and theory development* This is another important area where the voice of the people we are seeking to empower is to be heard and taken seriously. There are some examples of this happening, but clearly there is considerable scope for developing this further.

- *Political action* While there are clear contradictions and tensions for professional staff to be involved in political action (within their professional role at least), involvement in the personal capacity as private citizens is clearly not ruled out – and can, in fact, make a positive contribution. Empowerment, as we have noted, is a much broader political project than empowering professional practice. Service users can be supported to a certain extent in taking issues forward at a political level.

---

### Practice Focus 5.1

When the new degree programme was validated, the committee members were intrigued to note that service user involvement in the delivery of the course had been factored in to quite a significant extent. They wished the course team well with this bold approach but wondered whether they would encounter problems in putting their value commitment into practice. After the first year of the course had been completed, the staff group looked back and, while they recognised they had not achieved everything they set out to, they were very pleased that they had made a lot of progress in making user involvement a key part of the learning experience for students. They looked forward to building on this success in the coming year.

---

## Beyond tokenism

In recent years there has been an increasing emphasis across the human services on what has come to be known as 'user involvement' or 'user participation' or, in some cases, 'adopting a consumer perspective'. An example of this would be the PPI initiative in health care. This refers to the 'patient and public involvement initiative'. This is a scheme that was set up in England to try and promote a greater awareness of the perspective of people who use health care services. It has been a significant step forward in terms of giving users of health care services some degree of 'voice'. It is therefore a welcome move in terms of empowerment.

However, there is a danger that user involvement can become tokenistic. It can become a matter of professionals 'making the right noises' rather than genuinely involving users of services in the development, review, implementation and evaluation of services. We have to be very careful to guard against falling into this trap, as it can be very counterproductive. Indeed, we can see this as involving quite a disgraceful abuse of professional position to profess a commitment to empowerment through user involvement, but not to take any genuine responsibility to make this a reality (see Chapter 7). While workload pressures are often quoted as a reason for the commitment not being carried through, we have to recognise that this is not a legitimate reason for what amounts to abusing a position of professional trust.

There is a significant irony in terms of language use here. The term 'user' is one that has been heavily criticised for: (a) implying drug user, something which many users of health and welfare services are reluctant to have applied to them; and (b) the emphasis on service use implies a degree of passivity. It is therefore ironic that the term that has become established for involving the people we are trying to help, has become that of user involvement. However, this reflects a broader difficulty with language use. The widely used term, 'client' has been used less and less in social services contexts in the UK (although not elsewhere, and there is evidence that it is being used again more fully within the UK), but it continues to be used in other settings – for example, counselling. The term 'patient' is also problematic, in so far as, despite its continuing to be widely used, concerns have been raised about the suggestion that it too implies a degree of passivity. Clearly, these notions do not sit comfortably with the idea of empowerment.

## User involvement: some implications

User involvement is a matter of moving away from a traditional medical model. It is a process of involving people in dealing with their own problems and challenges and, as such, is a form of empowerment, especially as it is very strongly concerned with avoiding dependency creation. It has significant implications in terms of:

1. *Partnership* Working together relies on the people we are trying to help having a degree of voice ('power with', not 'power over'). If user involvement is not taken seriously, then the notion of partnership is severely undermined and can be seen as tokenistic. Again, it is a question of seeing the wider picture. User involvement and partnership working are part of a broader political project of empowerment, which in itself is part of a political commitment to promoting social justice, social inclusion and equality.
2. *Professionalism* As we shall see in Chapter 6, it is important that we move away from elitist conceptions of professionalism towards forms of professional relationships that are premised on partnership and empowerment. This, again, is clearly closely related to notions of user involvement, in so far as it is premised on shared agenda setting, rather than the professional taking a directive, 'top-down' approach.
3. *Supporting involvement* User involvement is not simply something that should be 'tolerated'. It can be an important and worthwhile professional role to support the development of user involvement – for example, by offering training on public speaking or other such relevant topics. As Baker *et al.* (2004) comment:

> Case studies of 'empowered participatory governance' in Porto Alegre in Brazil, Kerala in India and Chicago, Illinois all show that intensive training for participation can enable ordinary citizens to engage in participatory, deliberative decision-making (Abers, 1998, pp. 526–9; Baiochhi, 2003; Fung, 2003; Thomas Isaac and Heller, 2003). So, rather than worrying about citizens' limitations, we should be demanding more opportunities for participation supported by appropriate training. (pp. 102–3)

This is a neglected aspect of the situation that merits closer attention.

## Models of user involvement

There are many different models of user involvement. The following list is not comprehensive, but should provide you with a broad picture of some of the main approaches to user involvement:

- *The mental health survivor movement* This is an important movement in relation to attempting to move away from a medical model. It involves people who have experienced mental health problems, perceiving themselves as 'survivors' of the mental health system. This is a highly political approach which leads to a number of inherent tensions between the survivors and their carers. This is another example of the importance of language; the term 'survivor' (as opposed to 'patient') indicates that much of the problem is seen to lie within the mental health system itself and how a disempowering medicalised approach to mental health problems can be very destructive and counterproductive.
- *The disabled people's movement* Many disabled people have adopted a campaigning approach, focusing on 'rights not charity'. This means identifying the political bases of disability issues. This is a point to which we shall return in Chapter 11 where we discuss the social model of disability. Having a physical impairment does not have to mean being socially excluded, marginalised or disempowered.
- *Learning disabilities* In part, this movement is professionally driven, but is involved in challenging traditional professionalism. It is again part of the movement from elitist professionalism towards forms of professionalism premised on partnership and empowerment.
- *Older people* Unfortunately, this has been a neglected area. It is far less well developed than other areas. It is to be hoped that this will be a significant area of development in future. It is far too easy to fall into the stereotype that older people are somehow no longer part of mainstream society.
- *Children* The importance of listening to children and involving them in decision making (as part of growing up) has increasingly been recognised over time. We certainly need to move away from the Victorian idea that children should be seen and not heard – something that the children's rights movement has helped us to do in recent years. There is also the question of protecting children. Involving them in decision making and giving them greater control over their circumstances should not be equated with exposing children to responsibilities they are not ready for. (This is a good example of the balance we need in partnership, as discussed in Chapter 4.)

Empowerment is, of course, much wider than the professional arena. What we try to do in professional services and management is part of the much broader canvas of civil society and, indeed, of the political sphere of society as a whole. It would be naïve and unhelpful to see professional efforts to contribute to empowerment in isolation without recognising them as part of this much broader social and political movement of which user involvement forms a significant part. Croft and Beresford (2000) state that 'The professional definition of empowerment sees professional intervention as the route to service users' empowerment'

(p. 117). However, there is no reason to see professional intervention as *the* route to service users' empowerment. A more realistic view is to see it as one route among many.

---

### Practice Focus 5.2

Martin and Lana were pleased to have the opportunity to develop an advocacy project. They were both very committed to social justice and promoting people's rights, and so they welcomed the chance to develop advocacy services through the allocation of funding they had received for this scheme. However, when it came time to review the project after three months (one of the conditions of the funding), they were beginning to wonder whether they had misconceived the project. Their original aim was to use the opportunity to institute advocacy services for people who found it difficult (for a variety of reasons) to represent their own interests. But, through working with the people they had identified as potential users of such services, they had come to realise that a *self*-advocacy project would have been more appropriate – that is, a project geared towards supporting people in learning how to represent themselves (and only have somebody do it for them as a last resort). They acknowledged that they had made a mistake in not consulting potential service users in planning the project. They therefore decided to liaise with user-led organisations to try and reshape the project in a more empowering way.

---

## Conclusion

User involvement is a challenging development for professional practices that are carried out and managed along traditional lines. What needs to happen now is for service user involvement and the democratic principles in which it is based to become a more fully established part of mainstream practice. While people interested in elitism and privilege have much to fear from user involvement, critically reflective forms of practice committed to social justice can welcome it as a support for developing empowering approaches to service delivery.

Finally, it is worth emphasising that empowering forms of professional practice will need to value and support user-led organisations, even though at times there may be tensions and conflicts with such organisations. It is a very easy, but potentially disastrous, mistake to see some user involvement organisations as a problem because their approach to issues may not sit comfortably with a professional view. We have to avoid having the arrogance of assuming that, as professionals, we know best.

## Points to ponder

➤ How do you take account of user involvement issues in your practice?
➤ How can you build on this?
➤ What aspects of user involvement do you feel less comfortable with?
➤ How can you make progress with these?

# Chapter 6
# Professionalism

The significance of professionalism has already become established as an important theme of this book. The reason for this is that the idea of professionalism is in a process of change. Traditional approaches to professionalism can be shown to be not only unsympathetic to empowerment, but actually a major obstacle. However, what has emerged in recent years is a much more positive approach to professionalism which seeks to lose some of the unfortunate baggage of traditional approaches to what it means to be professional while retaining its strengths.

We are currently in a transitional period, in so far as there is a lot of evidence to show that traditional notions of professionalism are being left behind and replaced by more positive versions. However, there is also no shortage of evidence to show that the legacy of traditional professionalism is alive and well. We should therefore not be complacent and assume that the transition is one that has already taken place fully or will necessarily continue to happen smoothly. That would be a very naïve approach. The movement from traditional to new forms of professionalism is, in some respects, an ideological battleground, in so far as it involves abandoning long-established sets of power relations, and will no doubt continue to be so for some time to come. However, we can be positive in recognising that there have been significant steps forward. To explore these, I shall first of all outline the main elements of the traditional approach to professionalism. I will then give an overview of the new approach to professionalism that is steadily emerging. This will then set the scene for a discussion about how we can help to take forward this movement from old, disempowering approaches to professionalism to new, more positive ones that give much better scope for promoting empowerment.

## Traditional approaches to professionalism

According to the traditional model, a professional is someone who holds considerable power because he or she 'knows best'. This is based on the idea of professional expertise, the importance of an underpinning professional knowledge base. As we noted in Chapter 1, there are significant links between knowledge and power. This is captured in the idea that, for example, 'doctor knows best'. This is an example of medical discourse as discussed in Chapter 1. Foucault offers important comment here:

Medicine, as a general technique of health even more than as a service to the sick or an art of cures, assumes an increasingly important place in the administrative system and the machinery of power, a role constantly widened and strengthened throughout the eighteenth century. The doctor wins a footing within the different instances of social power. (in Faubion, 2002, p. 100)

A significant part of this model of professionalism is elitism, in the sense of regarding professionals as somehow 'above' others, particularly above the people who require our help. With this approach, it is not a partnership of equals when it comes to a professional working with a client/service user/patient. There is a very clear hierarchy involved, with the professional in the dominant position. While this can be helpful to professionals at times, it can be very unhelpful to those receiving help from the professional. It can also, ironically, be unhelpful to the professional in many circumstances, as such elitism can breed resentment, lack of co-operation and all the problems that can arise from that, such as hostility or even aggression or violence. It can also be problematic in so far as it can encourage passivity and even dependency. If the aim of the professional is simply to fulfil his or her wishes with the least amount of resistance, then passivity is something to be welcomed. However, if the professional is genuinely committed to helping and supporting, then such disempowering approaches are clearly problematic.

The professions of social work, nursing, youth and community work, and so on, are all historically part of what can be seen as a 'pseudo-medical' form of professionalism. We can see that contemporary human services practices have traditionally been based on a medical model, even where the primary concern of the intervention has not been of a medical nature. Consider for example the points raised in the following passage from Jones (1994):

In writing of *iatrogenesis* [Illich] is referring to the damage inflicted by doctors at the level of clinical misjudgement and negligence and to hospital-induced disease and injuries. A second stage identified is 'social iatrogenesis': that is, increased dependence on medical expertise leading to the medicalisation of aspects of life, blind belief in medical progress and the institutionalisation of medicine as an industry which commodifies and sells 'health'. The final stage, 'structural iatrogenesis', refers to the stripping away from human culture of ways of coping with birth, pain and death and their replacement by a sanitised, technological medical intervention against which individuals and societies are unable to fight back. People stop relying on and trusting each other and depend only on medical intervention. (p. 456)

The implications of this are far reaching in a number of ways. However, the particular issue I wish to focus on for present purposes is the comment about the 'medicalisation of aspects of life'. If social and personal and family problems are presented as part of a discourse of medicine (that is, seen as social 'ills' in more than a metaphorical sense), the likely response is one of passivity and dependency – waiting for the 'expert' to diagnose the problem and prescribe the solution. A more empowering model therefore needs to move away from this medical model of problems and (professional) solutions.

In some ways, traditional professionalism can be characterised by dominance or 'power over'. It is a relatively simple model in which the service user or patient is in straitened circumstances and reports problems, difficulties or unmet needs, while the strong, powerful and competent professional diagnoses the problem and offers a solution (see the quote from Moss, 2005 above). It is very clearly a top-down model.

---

**Practice Focus 6.1**

Olive quickly settled into her placement and felt that things were going well, although she did find some aspects of the work quite frustrating. However, she was surprised when her mentor told her he had concerns about how she was approaching her work. He said that he felt she was working out what people needed to do to solve their problems and was then becoming frustrated when they did not do it. He tried to get across to her that her role was not simply to 'diagnose' the problem and 'prescribe' the cure (and then get frustrated when they did not follow her advice or 'prescription'). He explained that it was much more about working together to identify what was wrong and how to improve the situation. If the people concerned felt they were being given 'instructions', it was not surprising they did not want to follow them. Olive was quite hurt by this criticism to begin with, but after further discussion, she started to see what had been happening and started to come round to the idea that she would need to rethink her approach.

---

## The new professionalism

In the new forms of professionalism that are emerging, knowledge is still important, but knowledge is seen as part of an ethos of partnership geared towards empowerment. It is not a case of creating a discourse of 'the professional knows best, based on his or her knowledge', but rather that the professional can make a contribution to partnership based on that knowledge. 'You are powerless because I am powerful' becomes 'we can be powerful together'.

New forms of professionalism are democratic, in the sense that it is not intended to be a top-down relationship between professionals and their clientele, but rather a situation where the two work together towards mutually agreed goals. The partners in the process are involved in a project of agreeing what the problems are, what the potential solutions are and how best to move forward.

In some circumstances (for example, those involving a high level of technical knowledge or skill) the professional may have a major contribution to make in terms of identifying what the problems and potential solutions are (for example, in terms of a medical diagnosis and prognosis). However, even in those situations, there is still considerable scope for people having a much stronger say in terms of their circumstances and how they are managed. The new approach to professionalism is one that gives people *voice*. This is part of the partnership approach discussed in Chapter 4. It may sometimes involve the need for negotiation, or even conflict management, skills, but that is the nature of democracy. It is still an important step forward compared with a traditional model based on the professional holding all the cards.

An important part of new approaches to professionalism is reflective practice. Fook (2002) captures the point well when she argues that:

> A critical reflective approach should allow . . . [practitioners] to interact with and respond to power dynamics in situations in a much more flexible, differentiated and therefore effective way. By making less 'blanket' assumptions about power, the critically reflective practitioner should be able to engage with the specific power dynamics of situations in more relevant and effective ways. (p. 157)

A key point here is the emphasis on working constructively with power dynamics rather than, as in the traditional model of professionalism, taking power relations for granted: 'The language of professionalism frequently serves to obscure the issue of power' (Hugman, 1991, p. 6). Reflective practice involves looking beneath the surface to see the complexities of the situation that might otherwise be overlooked. Power is just such a complexity, and it is far better that we engage with it in an informed way, rather than allow it to influence developments in line with traditional practices that put the professional in a position of dominance and thus contribute more to disempowerment than to empowerment.

New approaches to professionalism are geared toward encouraging self-help, growth and development, and are therefore a significant part of developing empowering forms of practice. Human services professionals in this new version of professionalism can be seen as *empowering* professionals rather than *dominating* professionals. This is significant in at least two main ways, in terms of:

(i) *values* It is impossible to square a commitment to equality and diversity with top-down professional approaches; and

(ii) *pragmatism* We have to question how much effectiveness an approach based on relations of dominance can have, compared with a partnership-based approach.

Westwood (2002) offers apt comment when she argues that power is not simply a matter of dominance. She quotes from Foucault (1978: 94) who wrote that:

> Power is not something that is acquired, seized or shared, something that one holds on to or allows to slip away: power is exercised from innumerable points, in the interplay of non-egalitarian and mobile relations. (p. 2)

This links well with the discussion of Power in Part One where it was emphasised that it is a complex matter often subject to oversimplification. A reflective, empowering professional is someone who is tuned into the complexities of power and aims to draw on these constructively and supportively to work towards agreed goals.

In this new approach, 'power with' is to the fore and is geared towards increasing 'power to' and 'power from within'. 'Power over' may have to apply in some circumstances (where statutory requirements apply, for example), but this should be seen as a last resort, rather than a fundamental basis of practice.

Barnes and Bowl (2001) capture the spirit of a reflective, empowering, partnership-based approach to professionalism when they comment that:

> A model of partnership practice which enables the knowledge and insights of both user and professional to be drawn on in developing problem-solving strategies not only has the potential to produce better outcomes for the user, it can also provide learning opportunities for professional actors to develop better practice (Marsh and Fisher, 1992). Both user and professional can benefit as a result. (p. 20)

---

### Practice Focus 6.2

Olive found the course on empowerment very challenging but also very rewarding. It helped her understand more fully why her mentor had been concerned when she was adopting a 'top-down' approach to her work. Following the discussions on the course and the examples of good practice given by the facilitator, she felt much more confident in trying to adopt a more empowering approach. She could see the value of professionalism but recognised that it needed to be an empowering 'power with' form of professionalism rather than a 'power over' traditional approach.

---

## Conclusion: From old to new

Making sure that the progress to date in moving from disempowering to empowering forms of professionalism continues is going to be a significant challenge for us. It will involve, for example, making sure that the lessons relating to working in partnership and promoting user involvement are fully learned and taken to heart. It will mean that we must focus on social justice, equality and diversity, as we shall emphasise in Part Three. It also involves recognising that knowledge must be used as a tool for helping, not as a means of separating or isolating people as part of a strategy of dominance. Foucault has shown us that knowledge and power go hand in hand, but the power that comes with knowledge does not have to be 'power over'. It is very much a matter of looking at how that knowledge and its power are used.

Servian (1996) offers helpful comment when he argues that:

> the possibility exists of power being used not *against* but *for* people. The exercise of power need not necessarily be oppressive. Indeed, the challenge to oppression can be seen as an object of having power. It can be strongly argued that the role of medical and non-medical professionals is meant in support of people 'in their care'.

Obviously, the reality may often be different, but this need not be an inevitability. In any case, in analysing power at all, the possibility is raised of challenging and using it. The answer remains how, and in what circumstances power is used for rather than against, and this may be helped through looking at psychological studies of individuals and at possible generalisations of strategies of protest. (p. 21)

It amounts to developing and sustaining a professionalism based on values such as:

- *equality and diversity* To make sure that our work is based on fairness and does not punish people for being different in some way;
- *respect and dignity* Being in positions of power does not give us, as professionals, the right to treat people disrespectfully or to undermine their dignity; and, of course,
- *empowerment itself* as a key value underpinning human services practice and management.

Ultimately, what we need to work towards is an *authentic* professionalism, one that is based on professional knowledge, accountability and values, but one which does not have an underpinning undermining focus on elitism, perks and professional distance.

## Points to ponder

➤ What ideas do you associate with the notion of 'professionalism'?
➤ Do your ideas need to change towards a more empowering form of professionalism?
➤ If so, how?
➤ What can you identify as the benefits of an empowering professionalism?

# Chapter 7
# Making empowerment real

Chapter 2 provided an overview of the theory base underpinning empowerment. Chapters 3 to 6 have cast further light on this by covering a range of important issues that underpin our efforts to promote empowering forms of practice. All of this is important when it comes to developing theoretically informed approaches to practice. But what is also important is being able to translate theory into practice – that is, developing reflective practice that draws on this theory base. This chapter cannot provide prescriptions for practice (nor would it be appropriate to do so), but what it can do is highlight some key issues to consider in rising to the challenge of making empowerment a genuine feature of practice, rather than just a rhetorical commitment that does not manifest itself in actual practice.

## Beyond reductionism

The subject of empowerment has been dogged for a very long time by the problem of 'faddism'. By this, what I mean is the tendency for the subject to be treated as a fad or fashion, and therefore treated in an oversimplified, tokenistic way without doing justice to the underlying complexities – and, in the process, doing a major disservice to the people we are seeking to help. This can be seen as part of a broader process of oversimplifying matters relating to discrimination, oppression and social justice. There is a lot of evidence to show that efforts to tackle discrimination and oppression have been characterised by oversimplification – no doubt, in large part caused by a high degree of defensiveness resulting from wave after wave of criticism for the neglect of such issues in previous years (Thompson, 2005b).

Brandon (2000) covers similar ground when he makes the important point that:

> Anti-discrimination strategies become ends in themselves, just mantras for use in college student assignments, separated from any genuine struggle against racism or sexism. We lose sight of the overall struggle for liberation. (p. 56)

What this means, therefore, is that we have to be very careful in thinking through the issues. We have to use our analytical skills in terms of, for example, asking ourselves when we use the term 'power': which form of power are we referring to? When we use terms like 'empowerment', what exactly do we mean by that? Empowerment, in what way? Using our analytical skills in this way is an important means of making sure that we do not fall into this trap of reductionism fuelled by a strong tendency towards anti-intellectualism in some branches of the human services (notably social work) and also management, education and development (Jones, 1996). It is therefore important to recognise that a genuine commitment to empowerment has a significant value – just paying lip service to it is clearly not enough. This chapter is therefore concerned with how we can move away from the tokenism of fashionable interest in empowerment and begin to make it a real issue for professional practice and management. Anything less would be an abuse of our professional position and the trust implicit within this.

In my view, this involves steering clear of common mistakes and the tendency towards oversimplification. In particular, I would suggest that we need to avoid three main fallacies and three main mistakes as follows:

## 1. Three fallacies

- *Power is necessarily bad or oppressive* We have noted from earlier discussions that this is again a gross oversimplification. 'Power over' may in certain circumstances, be oppressive and therefore clearly a bad thing. However, to regard all forms and usages of power as necessarily bad or oppressive is wildly inaccurate and extremely misleading. Faubion (2002) casts some light on this when he states that:

  > Foucault was interested . . . in showing that power 'comes from below', that is, that global and hierarchical structures of domination within a society depend on and operate through more local, low-level, 'capillary' circuits of power relationship. Another methodological principle was a refusal to treat 'power' as a substantive entity, institution, or possession, independent of the set of relationships in which it is exercised. (pp. xxiv–v)

  It is not simply a matter of two groups of people, powerful oppressors (professionals, for example) and the powerless oppressed (our clientele). As we saw in Chapter 1, the reality is far more complex and multi-layered than this.

  It is a great pity that this fallacy has become so well established, as it has the effect of significantly distorting the reality of power as something that can be positive or negative, a help or a hindrance (and sometimes both at the same time).

- *Empowerment involves giving away power* Power is not something that people can possess in a physical, tangible way. It is, to a large extent, about dispositions, institutionalised patterns, relationships and structures and, in order to appreciate the complexities of power and empowerment, we have to look at matters in a much more sophisticated way than just seeing empowerment as 'giving away' power. This very misleading, oversimplified approach can be very dangerous, although, unfortunately, it has become a widely adopted perspective.

- *Professional power is elitist* As we noted in Chapter 6, traditional forms of power certainly include a strong element of elitism. However, to reject professionalism altogether is, in effect, to throw the baby out with the bath water, because it is quite clear from modern developments in our thinking around professionalism that it is possible to be professional without being elitist. We can therefore be professional without setting up unhelpful top-down relationships. As we noted in Chapter 6, it is vitally important that we move away from elitist approaches to professionalism that promote paternalistic relations of dominance and to establish a much firmer basis of empowering professionalism. It is elitism that is the problem, not professionalism.

## 2. Three mistakes

- *Being complacent about power* As we have seen, power is a very complex issue, and it is understandable (but not acceptable) that some people would want to avoid the subject and hope that it will go away. This approach is captured in such comments as: 'I'm fed up with all this PC nonsense'. Such comments illustrate a reluctance to engage with the very real and very important issues of power and empowerment. We cannot afford to be complacent about such matters, although it is understandable that the oversimplified approach to these issues will have put many people off taking them seriously.
- *Being defeatist or cynical* Westwood (2002) comments on how widespread and multi-layered the operation of power is:

  > Giddens notes, according to the theory of structuration, 'Power is intrinsic to all interactions . . .' (ibid.). Thus emancipation is a flawed project in so far as there is no social space beyond authority. Instead, the best to work for is 'the achievement of rationally defensible authority' (Cassell, 1993: 228). (p. 17)

  This is an important passage, although much hinges on what is meant by 'emancipation'. If this is assumed to mean *complete* freedom from oppression, then that is something that is consistent with the approach taken in this book. However, if it is meant to suggest that oppression cannot be reduced or minimised through concerted attempts to do so, I would regard that as too defeatist a position to adopt.

  The comment that 'there is no social space beyond authority' is also an important one. It shows that we have to be aware of the significance of authority and ensure, as far as we reasonably can, that such authority is exercised responsibly, based on an explicit understanding of the complexities of power, rather than a naïve and complacent approach that brushes issues of power under the carpet.

  Adopting a defeatist approach to power is therefore uncalled for, as it is a very dangerous strategy to adopt.

- *Being unrealistic* Professional contributions to empowerment are only one small part of the wider political project of empowerment, social justice and social inclusion. As professionals and managers, we have a part to play, but we must not inflate our own importance. Realism means being neither defeatist nor naïvely overoptimistic. This is a wise way forward for us, steering a clear and important path between the unhelpful extremes of, on the one hand, seeing ourselves as 'knights on a white charger' in terms of empowering practice and, on the other, rejecting empowerment as an idealistic, unattainable goal. The reality is somewhere in between those two destructive extremes.

---

### Practice Focus 7.1

Sunita decided it would be a good idea to discuss empowerment at a staff development session, so she put it on the agenda. It turned out to be a very interesting and useful session, but she was very surprised by the range of views on the subject. Some people were quite negative and cynical about it, bordering on defeatism ('A lot of rhetoric but not much reality', as one person put it). At the other extreme, there were some people who became quite fired up about the subject and felt that this was the way forward. Sunita decided it would be important to be realistic about what could be achieved, partly to fend off the cynicism and partly to make sure that the initial enthusiasm did not burn out when the inevitable obstacles and complications arose.

---

It is extremely important that we do not allow empowerment to become reduced to an empty buzzword (Gomm, 1993). This would do a major disservice to a very important concept but, more importantly, it would do a major disservice to groups of people who are disadvantaged or oppressed in some way, as our mishandling of this concept could be a significant barrier to aspects of their progress. Again, we need to be very wary of the dangers of reductionism – of oversimplifying some very complex issues by looking for simple, definitive ways forward rather than engaging with the complexities in a critically reflective way.

Servian (1996) alerts us to the dangers of not engaging properly with the demands of empowerment when he reports on his own research:

> The findings of this study reinforce the views . . . that without positive and theoretically well-grounded ideas and methods of individual empowerment, organisational changes just reproduce traditional power relations. (p. 56)

As part of avoiding such oversimplification, we need to be clear about the terms we are using and what we mean by them. If we are not clear which form of power we are talking about (and therefore, by extension, what type of empowerment), we are likely to be confusing matters and thereby causing unnecessary problems – being part of the problem instead of part of the solution.

## Types of power, types of empowerment

In terms of the four different forms of power identified in Chapter 1, we can briefly sum up how empowerment can be made real in relation to each of these:

- *Power to* This involves maximising potential – for example, by providing information and helping people learn, providing reassurance and moral support, boosting confidence, helping to 'rewrite' destructive or oppressive narratives. There is tremendous scope for positive work here provided that mechanistic approaches are not allowed to squeeze this type of work out of the picture. This can be quite a challenge in some organisations – all the more reason for people to work together to promote empowering forms of practice, rather than leave it at the level of individual employees (and managers) working in an isolated way.
- *Power over* Here we can make sure that we keep this to a minimum, using authority only when necessary, legitimate and proportional (for example, to protect people from harm):
  - *necessary* It is a last resort; there is no other feasible means of dealing with the situation.
  - *legitimate* It can be justified in relation to an ethically appropriate assessment of what needs to be done.
  - *proportional* The degree of power used is proportional to the extent of concern – that is, it is not based on an overreaction or 'overkill'.

As Faubion (2002) puts it, it is a matter of: 'maximizing capacities while minimizing domination' (p. xxxiii). The reality of contemporary human services practice is that it would be naïve to think that there is no place for 'power over'. A significant part of professional accountability is making sure that 'power over' is kept to a minimum and, where it becomes necessary, exercised responsibly.

- *Power with* Working in partnership and supporting solidarity movements are clearly essential elements of this. As we have noted on more than one occasion, working together (with the people we are seeking to help, with carers and with professional colleagues – within our own organisation and beyond), is a fundamental basis for good practice.
- *Power from within* We can play an important part in facilitating this wherever possible – for example, by building on strengths and supporting the development of resilience. Professional practice (and indeed management) based on spirituality – in the sense of finding meaning – can be an important contributory factor in terms of helping people draw on their own strengths and inner resources. If people do not have sense of 'power from within', it is unlikely that they will feel comfortable with maximising their 'power to', resisting 'power over' and playing a positive role in 'power with'. It is ironic

that this aspect of empowerment that has traditionally featured very little in the literature on the subject can be seen to play a central role.

Promoting good practice involves working on all four of these fronts as far as possible, although it is clearly the case that some aspects will feature more than others at certain times. We need to beware, though, of finding one or more aspects easier to deal with and thus devoting more time to our favoured elements than to the overall picture.

---

### Practice Focus 7.2

Although Patrick had had a very religious upbringing, he was very interested in how people maintained a sense of meaning in their lives, with or without the aid of a religion or faith community. After reading about 'power from within' he realised he could look more closely in his work setting at how people tried to make sense of their circumstances and problems, whether these were to do with health difficulties, conflicts, bereavement or other losses or any other such matter. The more he looked into it, the more he found it both interesting and useful, casting light on various aspects of his work (for example, in terms of people's sense of identity and how this affected their levels of confidence, motivation and determination). He came to realise that 'power from within' was a greatly neglected aspect of the challenges he faced.

---

## Bringing about real change

In tackling all of these aspects of empowerment, we have to remember that:

> although empowerment is vital to successful . . . [practice], its position is uncertain, or *problematic*. At its strongest, it is a challenging concept pointing to the imperative for those who have least and are treated most unjustly in society to take power and rise up against that injustice, against the people and the structures which oppress them. At its weakest, it may be diluted or taken over altogether by professionals and others in powerful positions, so that it fits neatly and benignly into professional frameworks and does not change the ways people receiving services are controlled, managed, assessed and treated. (Adams, 2003, p. 4)

In seeking to make empowerment real we have to make sure that we are not just fine tuning existing arrangements, but rather, moving towards a more egalitarian approach to meeting people's social, personal and health needs. This is in many ways a major challenge, but the potential rewards are certainly worth the effort.

Barnes and Bowl (2001) offer a list of 'elements' of empowerment that could be used to form the basis of developing helpful practical strategies for taking empowerment forward. Space does not permit a detailed analysis of these (they could merit a chapter each), but they are none the less worth pointing out:

Empowerment can be considered to comprise:

- personal growth and development;
- transformation within social groups, for example, families;
- gaining greater control over life choices;
- increased influence over services received individually;
- increased influence in determining the nature of services available to all those sharing similar circumstances or characteristics;
- resistance to and subversion of dominant discourses and practices;
- gaining a presence within political systems from which you have been excluded;
- a means of achieving structural change: reducing inequalities;
- a means to health improvement;
- a process of developing and valuing different knowledges – linking knowledge and action – praxis (pp. 24–25)

Barnes and Bowl offer helpful ideas about how these can be addressed in a mental health context, although much of what they write can relatively easily be adapted to other settings.

## Conclusion

In a sense, this chapter is the heart of the book, in so far as it is concerned with drawing on the theory base underpinning empowerment and beginning to explore how the very real challenge of developing empowering forms of practice can be tackled. There are no easy answers, but it is to be hoped that the discussions presented here can at least take us in the right direction when it comes to trying to make a reality of the benefits that empowerment can bring.

## Points to ponder

➤ What can you do to help increase people's 'power to'?
➤ How can you make sure that 'power over' is used only when 'necessary, legitimate and proportional'?
➤ How can you contribute to making the most of 'power with'?
➤ What steps can you take to help people develop and draw on their 'power from within'?

# Part Three: Tackling Discrimination and Oppression

## Introduction

Discrimination and oppression can be seen to involve the misuse or abuse of power, and so any consideration of power needs to take account of these issues. Similarly, empowerment provides an important platform for tackling the myriad problems associated with processes of discrimination and the oppressive outcomes they lead to. Part Three is therefore concerned with how an understanding of power and empowerment can be brought to bear in rising to the challenge of developing anti-discriminatory practice and thereby promoting equality and valuing diversity.

Part Three comprises a series of seven short chapters, each addressing an area of discrimination. Chapter 8 focuses on gender and the significance of sexism. Chapter 9 concentrates on race and ethnicity and thereby seeks to lay a foundation for using empowerment as part of a commitment to anti-racism. Chapter 10 focuses on ageism, a topic that has attracted increasing attention since the introduction in October 2006 of regulations designed to tackle age discrimination.

Chapter 11 tackles disability discrimination issues and draws attention to the problems involved in adopting a medicalised approach and proposes a 'social' model in its place. Chapter 12 focuses on sexuality and the ways in which discrimination manifests itself in this regard. Chapter 13 explores how discrimination relating to religion plays a significant part in modern society and, finally, Chapter 14 considers inequalities relating to class, poverty and deprivation – important issues that also underpin the other areas of discrimination.

Part Three covers a broad range of issues. Space does not permit an in-depth analysis of these important issues (or, just as importantly, how they inter-relate as part of a more integrated understanding of discrimination and oppression). For that, you would be well advised to make good use of Part Four where guidance on further learning is offered.

# Chapter 8
# Gender

Gender is a very significant feature of social life, in so far as social reality is characteristically defined in terms of men. Women tend to be defined in relation to men. This is captured in Simone de Beauvoir's notion of 'alterity' or 'otherness'. The idea of the 'spare rib', of woman not having an identity in her own right except in relation to man:

> The terms *masculine* and *feminine* are used symmetrically only as a matter of form, as on legal papers. In actuality the relation of the two sexes is not quite like that of two electrical poles, for man represents both the positive and the neutral, as is indicated by the common use of *man* to designate human beings in general; whereas woman represents only the negative, defined by limiting criteria, without reciprocity. (de Beauvoir, 1972, p. 15)

Man is the norm, woman is 'other'. While we can continue to live and work in social structures and cultures that support such sexist notions, we will struggle to make major progress in terms of empowerment in relation to gender. However, this is not to say that no progress can be made at all, but we do have to be realistic.

## Gender inequalities

Traditionally, sexism is seen as a matter exclusively affecting women and, indeed, is often defined specifically as discrimination against women. This reflects the fact that, in terms of both quality and quantity, gender discrimination affects women far more than men. However, it would be both inaccurate and unhelpful to assume that gender-related discrimination never applies to men. The upshot of this is that both women and men can suffer as a result of, for example, gender stereotypes. Empowerment in relation to gender therefore relates to all human beings, not just to women. Women can certainly be held back by gender stereotypes that present them as primarily carers in the domestic sphere and undermine any efforts to establish themselves in the public sphere of work and/or public life. However, gender stereotypes can also hold some men back, at least in terms of unhelpful stereotypes that cast them in the role of hunter, aggressor or other such role that can be a source of significant discomfort. This is not to say that men have as much to gain from challenging sexism as women do, but it is important to recognise that the situation is more complex than the simple idea of men as oppressors and women as the oppressed.

In relation to gender, we can understand empowerment in terms of the three levels of PCS analysis (Thompson, 2006c) as follows:

## *Personal*

Individuals can be easily 'seduced' by gender inequalities, in the sense that we are so used to them as part of our everyday lives that we often accept them unthinkingly – they are like comfortable shoes. They are so ingrained in our sense of normality that attempting to move beyond them can cause some degree of insecurity (see the discussion of 'ontological security' in Thompson, 2003a). Challenging gender can therefore be a source of anxiety for many people (women as well as men). Having the courage to tackle gender inequalities can be a significant part of 'power from within'.

## *Cultural*

The use of language is a central part of culture, in so far as:

1. it is through language that cultural assumptions are transmitted from one generation to the next; and
2. language influences us profoundly by shaping our sense of reality.

An example of how significant language can be in terms of gender is to be found in the following passage from the popular travel writer, Bill Bryson (1990):

> I come from Des Moines. Somebody had to.
> When you come from Des Moines you either accept the fact without question and settle down with a local girl named Bobbi and get a job at the Firestone factory and live there for ever and ever, or you spend your adolescence moaning at length about what a dump it is and how you can't wait to get out, and then you settle down with a local girl named Bobbi and get a job at the Firestone factory and live there for ever and ever. (p. 3)

I have used this passage as part of a training course on many occasions by displaying the quote on screen and then asking the group of participants what their reaction is to the particular statements made. It is interesting to note that the majority of participants do not have any specific reaction, and it is only a minority who point out that Bryson's use of language assumes that, in discussing the residents of the town, only the male perspective is important: 'when you come from' is referring to 'when a man comes from' (unless women in Des Moines also settle down with a girl called Bobbi). This is an example of how language constructs reality in male terms, thereby placing women in a secondary position. It is also an example – as illustrated by the fact that so many course participants over the years (women and men) have not initially spotted the gender bias in the language until it is pointed out to them – of how deeply ingrained such language forms are. This type of gender bias in language is a strong part of western cultures.

A further example of gender inequalities being ensconced in language is to be found in the following passage from Bachrach and Baratz (1970):

> Of course power is exercised when *A* participates in the decisions that affect *B*. Power is also exercised when *A* devotes his energies to creating or reinforcing social and political values . . . (p. 7, cited in Lukes, 2005, p. 20)

The fact that the authors use the terms 'his' and 'he' to refer to *A* is an example of how language can have the effect of excluding (and thus devaluing) particular groups or categories of people (in this case, women). This is an example of how subtle the workings of power can be at the cultural level.

---

### *Practice Focus 8.1*

Amy had been struggling with recruitment issues for some time. Her centre found it difficult to attract applicants for vacant posts in general, but in particular, they struggled to recruit women: 'Not enough applicants, and especially not enough women applicants' is how she put it at a management meeting. The problem was so serious that, at this meeting, the decision was made to seek the advice of a human resources consultant. This proved to be very worthwhile, as the perspective of an outsider with a wide understanding of practices in other organisations enabled her to advise that Amy and her colleagues needed to look at making the centre's culture less 'macho'. The consultant, after spending some time at the centre, pointed out that the language used, the subtle 'unwritten rules' of the culture and the taken-for-granted assumptions were all very masculine and would be off-putting to most women and, indeed, for quite a few men. Amy found this very helpful and set about looking at how best to bring about the changes needed.

---

There is also, within the cultural level, the issue of women being located predominantly within the private sphere and men in the public sphere. One of the implications of this is that women in paid caring roles (for example, within the human services) will often have their contribution devalued because it is seen as just an extension of their natural role. It is therefore important to go beyond stereotypical gender roles, as these can be highly problematic. For example, there is a great deal of evidence to show that there are gender-related patterns of grieving. If we do not take account of these differences, we may not be in a position to provide appropriate help to people when they need it most. Martin and Doka (2000) describe two patterns of grieving:

> One is an intuitive pattern where individuals experience and express grief in an affective way. In this pattern, grieving individuals will find adaptive strategies that are oriented toward the expression of affect. But there is another pattern as well, one that we label instrumental. Here, grief is experienced physically, such as a restlessness or

cognition. Here the adaptive strategies individuals use tend to be . . . cognitive and active as well.

This instrumental pattern is typical of the way many men grieve, due to contemporary patterns of male socialization. (p. 2)

What this illustrates is that, due to patterns of upbringing, men are more likely to feel comfortable with active, instrumental styles of grieving, while women are more likely to feel comfortable with styles that involve expressing emotion (affect). However, in each specific situation, it would be necessary to assess the style of grieving the individual concerned feels more comfortable with, rather than fall into gender stereotypes by assuming that *all* men prefer instrumental styles while *all* women prefer expressive ones.

### Structural

An example of gender issues at the structural level is in terms of institutionalised patterns of inequality – for example, the 'glass ceiling', as it is commonly known, that can be such a key factor in preventing women from rising to management positions, especially senior management positions (Wirth, 2000). What we can learn from looking at the structural level in terms of gender is that society is not a level playing field. There are inbuilt inequalities and disadvantages, especially for women in how our society is organised.

## Promoting empowerment

We should not underestimate how deeply ingrained disempowering gender inequalities are and how well 'camouflaged' they can be by so-called 'common sense' assumptions. It is therefore important to get past surface impressions and appreciate the underlying complexities and subtleties. In particular, it is very important to avoid tokenistic and patronising approaches. It is interesting (and also sad) to note that many men and some women respond to discussion of gender inequalities with nervous laughter and will often try and dismiss these issues as trivial. Given that gender is something that applies to all of us, there is potentially considerable motivation to make sure that society's rules about gender are not such that they act as a barrier to empowerment. More realistically, we can recognise that empowerment in relation to gender is a key part of the social justice agenda.

## Points to ponder

> In what ways do gender differences apply to your line of work?
> How can you avoid reinforcing gender stereotypes?
> What steps can you take to promote empowerment in relation to gender?

# Chapter 9
# Race and ethnicity

It should come as no surprise to anyone to recognise that racism is a significant barrier to empowerment. Racism is, of course, a degrading matter. It involves treating people as less than human (consider, for example, the history of slavery). If we are to be serious about promoting empowerment, we therefore have to give a great deal of attention to the importance of anti-racism. We need to make sure that a person's ethnic identity can be a source of pride and not a reason for being discriminated against, abused or mistreated.

In developing empowering forms of practice, it would be naïve in the extreme not to take account of the significance of racism in the lives of many of the people we seek to help. As noted earlier, some reductionist approaches to issues of ethnicity, race and racism have had the effect of making many people reluctant to engage with these complex and sensitive issues. However, if we are to make a reality of empowerment, we need to put such problems behind us and develop more sophisticated understandings of the issues, so that people can more readily appreciate the importance of taking anti-racism seriously.

## The effects of racism

We can recognise that racism has the effect of:

- *Denying opportunities* Racism is a significant part of social exclusion, denying opportunities to people from ethnic minorities in a wide variety of settings and circumstances. This is not simply a matter of a minor level of unfairness that can be dismissed with comments like: 'Well, life can't be totally fair'. It can be a serious source of oppression to people who are denied significant opportunities on spurious grounds of 'race' or ethnicity.
- *Treating people as inferior* A major part of racism is the assumption of white superiority. This dangerous fallacy can be internalised by some people, with very disempowering effects (although, as we noted in our discussion relating to resilience in Chapter 3, this is not always the case). A notion of white superiority has been so deeply ingrained in dominant cultures for so long that it is often the case that white people are reflecting this point of view without even realising that they are doing so. A reliance on widely used negative stereotypes of minority ethnic groups can be a significant part of this.
- *Stigmatising* People can be made to feel ashamed for being members of certain minority ethnic groups even though there is no objective justification

for this. This travesty of justice is sadly not uncommon. It follows on as a natural consequence of the assumption of white superiority. Attaching a negative label to people on racial or ethnic grounds clearly has no place in forms of practice and management premised on empowerment. Indeed, I would argue that a key part of empowering practice is to challenge such stigmatisation.

- *Undermining educational achievement* Racism can have a very detrimental impact in terms of education (Dadzie, 2000). This can have a 'domino effect', in so far as educational inequalities can have implications for employment, housing and various other aspects of social experience. The racism inherent in the education system is therefore a major barrier to equality. Empowering forms of practice need to take account of this unfair bias in the educational dimension of people's lives.

All these, and many others we do not have space to refer to, add up to a very considerable source of disempowerment. Clearly, racism is a major obstacle to empowerment, although it can indeed be a stimulus to empowerment as a fighting response to the injustices involved.

---

**Practice Focus 9.1**

Sheila had worked in a predominantly white area in her previous post. However, in her new job she found that about twenty per cent of the people she was trying to help were from minority ethnic backgrounds. She had previously been aware of racism and the need to tackle it. However, it had always been a relatively minor consideration in the overall scheme of things. Now, however, it was rapidly becoming a central part of her work as she came across example after example of racial discrimination. She felt a bit overwhelmed to begin with, but soon realised she would have to rise to the challenge, as her sense of social justice would not allow her to neglect the problems of racism she could now see so clearly. After a while she also started to realise that she could have done a lot more to promote racial equality in her previous post. She wondered whether complacency had allowed the issues to become marginalised.

---

## Tackling racism

From the comments above, we can see that promoting empowerment clearly needs to involve tackling racism. This is a broad-ranging undertaking that needs to be approached on a number of fronts. This includes the following:

- *Avoiding and challenging racial stereotypes* This involves unlearning (and helping others to unlearn) much of what our cultural upbringing will have taught us. It is sometimes surprising to note how deeply ingrained stereotypes can be within cultural assumptions and dominant discourses. Such racial stereotypes can be very harmful, as they distort reality.

- *Valuing diversity* We need to move away from 'ethnocentricity', the tendency to define reality narrowly in terms of our own ethnic background and, in doing so, to devalue other cultures and perspectives. The notion of valuing diversity is a much more positive approach that concerns itself with appreciating the benefits that ethnic and other forms of diversity bring to society.
- *Being aware of, and challenging, institutional racism* This would include, for example, challenging policies that fail to address the needs of people from ethnic minorities. It is not enough to avoid overtly racist actions and language; we also have to be aware of how deeply ingrained in institutional patterns racism can be. This is parallel with Foucault's notion of power as institutionalised patterns of language and action – institutional racism manifests itself as a set of established power relations, with black people consistently assigned to subordinate positions, if not excluded altogether. Westwood (2002) captures this point well when she argues that:

> A Foucaldian account of racism is consistent with Stuart Hall's notion of race as a floating signifier, given meaning through the discourses and practices within which it is embedded. Thus, race is constantly worked upon, changed, re-ordered and made intelligible within the social, and it provides a key point for understanding the ways in which the social is constructed and comes to deconstruct the binary between the natural/biological and the social. (p. 35)

Empowerment is a complex issue in general, but when we look at how empowerment interacts with issues of race and ethnicity, the situation becomes even more complex. It is therefore necessary to make sure that we study this topic in depth and do not gloss over it. It is not enough to simply 'make the right noises' in a tokenistic response to pressures to challenge racism. This can be a highly emotive and, for some people, threatening subject, and so it is understandable that some people will want to push it to one side or sweep it under the carpet. However, the issues are far too important for that, and so we need to make sure that we are prepared to give these concerns our full attention. You are therefore strongly advised to follow up some of the references in Part Four.

## Conclusion

Race and ethnicity are pervading features of social life. It is therefore unwise, dangerous and unethical to fail to pay adequate attention to the significant elements of disempowerment that arise from racial inequalities. We need to make sure that we are able to achieve the positive and constructive balance between the two negative and destructive extremes of:

1. *Minimisation* This involves playing down the significance of racial discrimination, treating tackling racism as a minor matter, rather than a central plank of an organisation's strategy for promoting equality and valuing diversity.

2. *Too narrow a focus* In the early days of anti-racism, a commitment to ensuring that the issues were taken seriously led to racial discrimination being prioritised over other forms of discrimination. For example, the term 'anti-racist and anti-discriminatory practice' was widely used in the 1980s, as if anti-racism were not part of a broader political and professional project. It is now much clearer that we need to see anti-racism as part of a commitment to equality and diversity across various fronts and not an isolated undertaking. This is very important because racism interacts with other forms of discrimination in subtle but important ways and it would be a significant mistake not to take account of that.

Empowering forms of practice must therefore avoid these extremes by developing a fuller, more well-developed picture of how racism can have profoundly disempowering effects.

## Points to ponder

➤ Can you identify ways in which racial discrimination may feature in your line of work?

➤ What opportunities do you have for working together with others to tackle racism?

➤ What steps can you take to be empowering in relation to race and ethnicity?

# Chapter 10
# Age

Discrimination on the grounds of age is so well established that it is generally taken for granted and not noticed. It is as if it has become part of the wallpaper, as it were. An example of this is the fact that no legislation relating to age discrimination appeared in the United Kingdom until 2006. This lack of attention to age discrimination does not mean that it is not important. On the contrary, it shows how deeply ingrained it is and how powerful it is in its effects. As Sue Thompson (2005) puts it:

> ageism is a process that makes it seem acceptable or legitimate to discriminate on the grounds of one factor – a person's age. That is to say it allows us to think about whole groups of people purely in terms of their age, regardless of other factors such as ability, experience, social and cultural background or personality, and to treat them differently and often less favourably because of that perception. (p. 1)

This deeply ingrained nature of ageism shows how much of a challenge it is to tackle the disempowering effects of age discrimination.

## Age as a barrier

Age discrimination can apply to: (1) children and young people; and (2) older people; or (3) indeed anyone at any stage of the life course. Discrimination on the grounds of age can be very general, but it does tend to apply especially to people in groups (1) and (2) – that is, people at the extremes of the life course, the early stages and the latter stages.

A central part of age discrimination is the fact that children, young people and older people tend to be 'invisible' (or, to be consistent, with the notion of 'voice', perhaps we should say 'silent' rather than invisible). That is, they tend to be marginalised, with their needs not identified or addressed as fully as others. This lack of voice is therefore clearly a significant source of disempowerment. When it comes to decision making, for example, it is commonly assumed by many that people at the extreme ends of the life course will have less of a say than others. Over the years I have encountered example after example of this, especially in relation to older people – as if reaching a certain age invalidates a person's right to make their own decisions and thus have a say in matters relating to their health, well-being and social circumstances. Nusberg (1995) makes apt comment when she argues that:

Older people are one of the last groups with which the notion of empowerment has become associated. Yet the privileges it represents – the ability to make informed choices, exercise influence, continue to make contributions in a variety of settings, and take advantage of services – are critically important to the well-being of the elders. These are choices often taken for granted by working-age adults, but they have eluded older persons for a variety of reasons, including poverty, poor health, low educational levels, lack of transportation and access to services, negative stereotypes about aging, and overt and subtle age discrimination. As the world's population lives longer and more independent lives, it is clear that having choices and maintaining control over personal decisions has taken on new meaning and importance for older persons everywhere. (p. ix)

This is an important and significant passage, but it is surprising that Nusberg refers to the 'privileges' of making informed choices, exercising influence and continuing to make contributions. Surely these are rights rather than privileges.

## Disengagement and exclusion

In relation to older people, age discrimination manifests itself in the fact that it is often assumed that they should be disengaged from society. It is even encouraged by some people or seen as natural. Books have been written on the idea that older people should prepare for disengaging (see, for example Cumming and Henry, 1961). This in itself is a form of social exclusion, an example of marginalisation, as mentioned above. Why should it be assumed that older people no longer have a place in mainstream society? This reflects the dominant discourse relating to older people which is clearly one that contains a strong element of this notion of 'disengagement'.

Similarly, children and young people are often not seen as legitimate partici-pants in decision making (see Chapter 5). They are expected to be on the periphery of what are seen as adult matters. Indeed, relating back to older people, it is interesting to note that older people are often not referred to as adults. Consider, for example, a tendency to divide services in terms of Children's Services, Services for Adults and Services for Older People (or 'the elderly'). Is this simply a quirk of language or does it reflect a more deep-seated cultural attitude of marginalisation and exclusion of older people? The consistency with which older people are presented as peripheral to mainstream society tends to favour the latter interpretation.

## Tackling age discrimination

In terms of tackling age discrimination in relation to children and young people, the question of empowerment needs to be handled carefully and sensitively and not uncritically. As suggested in Chapter 5, it is important not to deprive children of their childhood by giving them responsibilities that they are not yet ready for.

Indeed, that could be seen as a form of abuse. However, despite these sensitivities, it is still important to consider how we can help children and young people to learn adult skills to be engaged in empowerment, rather than 'wrapped in cotton wool' because of their tender years. This is a significant challenge for everyone who works with children and young people.

When it comes to helping older people to empower themselves, a significant issue is the movement from dependency to interdependency. This means helping older people to be as independent as possible and not assuming that, because of their age, they will necessarily need to be dependent on others. That is a matter for assessment, not assumption. That is, we should not rely on stereotypes of dependency but, rather, actually take the trouble to work out in each situation we deal with how much (or how little) assistance an older person may need. Simply equating old age with dependency, with all the disempowerment this entails, is clearly not acceptable.

There is also the issue of 'killing' people with kindness to be considered. It is often the case that genuine efforts to protect and support people can have the unintended consequences of stifling and undermining. This applies to children and young people as well as to older people. If we take too protective an approach, we can do more harm than good. We can, in effect:

- cause resentment and ill-feeling;
- deskill people and undermine their confidence;
- demoralise and possibly contribute to depression; and
- waste scarce resources – thus leading to other people missing out on the help they need.

All these contribute more to disempowerment than empowerment.

Helping people who are subject to age discrimination is challenging work because this form of discrimination has yet to achieve the public attention that, for example, racism and sexism have had over the decades. Despite this lack of public awareness, there is still a lot that can be achieved by taking forward a commitment to trying to make sure that people are not disempowered simply because of their date of birth.

---

### Practice Focus 10.1

Ffion had worked with young people for many years and had become a very knowledgeable and skilful worker. However, she found it quite a challenge when she had a new line manager who was very committed to empowerment. At first she did not see it as an issue, as she was familiar with the idea of empowerment and saw it as an important part of helping children grow up. However, she soon began to realise that the model of empowerment being put forward by her new boss was much more far reaching, including challenging stereotypes of age-appropriate behaviour. While she felt uneasy about this to begin with, she realised that this could be an important step forward in terms of raising standards of practice.

Age discrimination has much in common with other forms of discrimination, such as sexism and racism. However, it is significantly different from them, in so far as differential treatment of people in accordance with their age not only goes largely unchallenged, it is also seen as desirable in many ways. People are expected to 'act their age', and will often encounter considerable disapproval if they do not fit in with socially constructed expectations of age-appropriate behaviour. This can have significantly disempowering effects, especially for older people who are likely to face a significantly restricted range of activities that are considered socially acceptable for 'the elderly'. This can be particularly significant in terms of 'power from within', in so far as being held back by social conventions that restrict according to arbitrary notions of age could significantly undermine confidence and personal resourcefulness.

## Points to ponder

➤ How do age issues relate to your field of work?
➤ How can you ensure that you are not relying on ageist stereotypes?
➤ What steps can you take to challenge disempowerment arising from age discrimination?

# Chapter 11
# Disability

Disability is another field that has a history of a paternalistic 'we know best' approach that is not a firm foundation for empowerment. However, the traditional approaches have been heavily criticised in recent years for holding disabled people back unnecessarily. When it comes to empowerment, the legacy of traditional practices we have is not a helpful one to hold onto. Progress therefore depends on developing new understandings of disability.

## The social model of disability

The traditional medicalised approach to disability has tended to emphasise what disabled people cannot do, and can therefore be seen as an unduly negative approach to the subject. It has also been criticised for reinforcing notions of dependency, as this is, of course, an inevitable consequence of such a negative outlook.

In addition, such approaches have been criticised for being too individualistic and for not taking account of social issues – especially the fact that it is society's reaction to physical impairments that have the effect of disabling. This conception of disability is what is known as the 'social model'. It is summarised well in the following passage from Hughes (2004):

> When UPIAS [Union of Physically Impaired Against Segregation] (1976) described the principles of what was to become the social model of disability, it did so by making a clear distinction between impairment and disability. Disability became defined as social oppression and impairment became associated with bodily pathology. The distinction had the effect of removing impairment and the body from disability discourse and of undermining the credibility of the medical model. The idea that disability was a form of sickness, the outcome of which was dependency and the need for rehabilitation was contested. The new perspective suggested that disability was a problem of social organisation (Oliver, 1990). The solution to the problem of disability, therefore, did not lie in clinical tinkering with 'broken bodies' but in systematic social change. (p. 63)

An example of the social model would be a situation in which a wheelchair user can be seen to be *dis*abled by the lack of appropriate access facilities (ramp, lift, and so on), rather than by his or her physical impairment. Similarly, a person with a visual impairment may have no difficulty using a lift that has Braille alongside the buttons for choosing a floor, but may be unable to use a lift that does not have this facility. It is the lack of attention to disabled people's needs in the design of buildings and facilities that causes the problems, rather than whatever physical impairment the person concerned may have. The attitudes underpinning such design problems can also be seen to apply more broadly, in so far as they reflect a discourse that places disabled people outside of mainstream society.

The development of the social model of disability has been quite a radical departure from traditional, medicalised approaches – that is, approaches that define disabled people primarily in terms of their physical impairments. It has emphasised that the problems disabled people experience are primarily a matter of social organisation and social expectations. In this way it introduces a sociological dimension. This is quite significant in terms of empowerment, as it means that any barriers to progress that disabled people experience are likely to owe as much to social factors, if not more so, than to their actual physical impairment. The social model seeks to challenge, for example, disabling assumptions, such as the notion that somebody with a learning disability cannot hold down anything but a very menial job. The disabled people's movement has played a major part in changing society's attitudes towards disability, although clearly there is still a long way to go yet. Traditional models are still dominant, despite the heavy criticisms that have come from the social model of disability and its proponents – although it is to be hoped that this will change over time as the social model becomes more established (in professional education and training, for example).

As with age discrimination, people with disabilities can be 'killed' with kindness; hence the use of the slogan of 'rights, not charity'. If we focus on empowerment, helping people to be as independent and self-sufficient as possible, then care needs can be addressed as part of this. However, if we focus primarily on care needs, it is very easy for us to fall into a paternalistic model that actually stands in the way of empowerment. This is not to say that professionals in the human services should not be concerned with care issues; that would clearly be nonsensical. What we should be concerned with, however, is making sure that empowerment is a priority, so that a focus on care needs does not become counterproductive by blocking access to pathways of empowerment.

---

### Practice Focus 11.1

Rosa was very hard working and very keen to do a good job. People commented on how committed she was and how she 'had a heart of gold'. It therefore came as a surprise to everyone, including Rosa herself, when a complaint was received. It related to her doing things for people that they were capable, perhaps with a little bit of support and patience, of doing for themselves. She felt devastated by the criticisms that had been made of her. As far as she was concerned, it was her job to look after people, and that is exactly what she had been doing. She was clearly going to need a lot of help to understand that making people dependent was not a caring thing to do.

Many people within the disabled people's movement see professionals as part of the problem. This is understandable, given the way traditional forms of professionalism have been open to criticisms of being patronising and for focusing on negatives without recognising:

(a)  the positive strengths that disabled people bring and their resilience – this is part of the notion of *interdependence*, the idea that people with disabilities have much to contribute and are not simply to be passive recipients of care; and

(b)  the fact that it is often misguided professional interventions and wider social attitudes that have played a central role in disempowering disabled people over a long period of time.

If we are to take empowering practice seriously, we need to make sure that our approach to disability is influenced by social model perspectives and is not allowed to be reduced to the problems generated by an oversimplified, medicalised approach.

## Working together

The disabled people's movement has played a major role in politicising disability issues and putting user involvement firmly on the agenda. By emphasising the importance of including the perspective of the service user, this political movement has had a significant influence on human services practice, especially in terms of the development of partnership working. A key part of empowerment in working with disabled people is therefore to remember the lessons learned about working together and thus actively including service users in the process of helping as equal partners – an approach far removed from traditional notions of elitist professionalism.

## Conclusion

The field of disability studies has changed enormously since the development of the social model of disability. Practice and management in the field, however, have not always kept up. The current picture is a very mixed one, in so far as there is clear evidence of new perspectives influencing policy and practice, but also, sadly, traditional disempowering aspects of practice remain firmly in evidence in many quarters. The challenge we face, then, is doing everything we reasonably can to build on the progress made and to move away from the aspects of practice that retain a paternalistic element. It is a significant challenge, but an important one if we are to be serious about developing empowering forms of practice.

## Points to ponder

➤ Can you identify the main differences between a medicalised approach to disability and a social model?

➤ What are the implications of a social model for your practice?

➤ What steps can be taken to move away from disempowering approaches to disability?

# Chapter 12
# Sexual identity

A person's sexual identity is a fundamental part of his or her sense of self. For that identity to be invalidated or treated as inferior, pathological or otherwise problematic, based on narrow and prejudicial conceptions of what constitutes 'appropriate' sexuality is clearly oppressive. In terms of empowerment in relation to sexual identity, we need to recognise, then, that we start from a very low baseline, in the sense that evidence of discrimination (and thus disempowerment) on the grounds of sexuality is widespread – the problems are deeply ingrained as part of a discourse of inequality that is part and parcel of cultural formations. What we face, then, is another major challenge.

## The relevance of sexual identity in the human services

On many occasions I have encountered a certain amount of resistance to engaging with issues of equality in relation to sexual identity. For example, on several training courses I have run, some participants have put forward the argument that they see no reason why sexuality should be included on the professional agenda in relation to equality. They can understand, they tell me, why ageism and disablism, for example, are considered important because it is part of the brief of social services, health care and so on to address the needs of older and disabled people. But, they ask, what has a person's sexual identity got to do with it? A good answer to this question is to be found in the work of Carabine (2004a) when she makes the very telling point that:

> Significantly, social policy does not have to be specifically concerned with sexuality for it to 'speak' of sexuality and for it to regulate sexual relations and behaviour. Social policies about, for example, housing, health, education, social exclusion, income support or parenting can also contain assumptions and convey messages about acceptable and normal sexual relations and practices as taking place within a two-parent, married family. . . . What we do sexually, our sexual relationships and how we experience our sexuality. In policy, welfare analyses and practice, sexuality is usually taken as given, as something that 'just is', and welfare subjects are assumed to be universally heterosexual. The idea of heterosexuality is left unproblematized and unquestioned. (pp. 2–3)

This important passage makes the point well that issues of sexuality are relevant to many aspects of the human services – although the fact that this is seldom recognised shows how discourses about so-called normal sexuality are dominant features of cultural understandings of these important issues.

Sexual identity and related issues are very relevant in terms of various sets of issues, not least the following:

- *Fostering and adoption* Prejudicial assumptions that alternative sexual identities preclude good parenting can lead to many complications.
- *Development of sexual identity* An important part of adolescent development. Although the development of a gay, lesbian or bisexual identity is not in itself problematic, facing the pressures of a discriminatory society can be.
- *HIV and AIDS* Although these are not exclusively matters of sexuality, they can have significant implications in relation to sexual identity.

## Heterosexism

The technical term for discrimination on the grounds of sexual orientation is 'heterosexism', although the term 'homophobia' (fear of, or hostility towards, homosexuality – that is, same sex relationships) is also widely used. This is a form of discrimination that operates at a personal level (personal prejudice); a cultural level (for example, in terms of stereotypes and the use of discriminatory language forms); and a structural level (for example, gay men, lesbians and bisexuals experiencing social exclusion and assigned an inferior status compared with the heterosexual majority).

A key ideological theme underpinning discrimination in its various forms is that of a discourse of naturalness as opposed to unnaturalness. That is, those aspects of life that are seen as positive and ideologically acceptable are regarded as 'natural', while those aspects that are disapproved of are dismissed as 'unnatural' – for example, within a discourse of sexism, it is assumed that it is 'natural' for men to play a dominant role. In this regard, heterosexuality is generally presented as 'normal' and thus as natural and positive. Other forms of sexuality are characteristically presented as abnormal, unnatural and thus negative and to be avoided. The use of this discourse of naturalness (or what Carabine, 2004a, calls 'heteronormativity') is a very powerful way of stigmatising what can be called alternative forms of sexuality. It presents heterosexuality as the only acceptable approach to matters of sexual relations and sexual identity. There is clearly a major basis of discrimination – and thus disempowerment – involved in this.

## Valuing diversity

Given the importance of valuing diversity, we should note that diversity should also be seen to apply to matters of sexuality. It is clearly the case that people should not be stigmatised or discriminated against on the grounds of their sexual identity or orientation if we are to be serious about our commitment to social justice and empowerment. It can be argued that attitudes have improved over time. For example, same sex relationships are no longer classified as symptoms of a 'mental illness', but there remains extensive evidence of prejudice and discrimination. As in so many other areas of discrimination, we still have a very long way to go.

It is important not to disempower people further by regarding non-heterosexual sexuality as 'deviant' or a problem. The problem is not alternative sexualities, but rather, irrational discrimination in relation to such non-mainstream preferences and cultural assumptions that present such discrimination as acceptable.

It is important to establish diverse sexualities as legitimate, and not something that needs to be hidden away. We cannot realistically profess a commitment to promoting empowerment while also subscribing to a view of sexuality that restricts what is acceptable to a socially constructed norm of so-called natural behaviour.

---

### Practice Focus 12.1

Dave had never worked with an openly gay patient before. It did seem a little strange at first, but he felt it presented no problems for him, as he had never subscribed to a discriminatory view of same-sex relationships. However, he was taken aback – and actually quite disappointed – by some of the comments made by some of his colleagues, who seemed to think that this person's sexual identity was something to laugh about. 'We're only joking, what's the matter with you?' was the response he received when he expressed his objections. He found it quite incredible that a team of people who were quite committed to equality in some ways did not seem to include sexual identity on their agenda of issues to be addressed – so deeply ingrained was the culture of seeing same-sex relationships as 'deviant'.

---

## Strategies for promoting empowerment

Carabine (1996) talks of strategies that can be used to promote empowerment in relation to sexuality. She focuses on three in particular:

- *Empowerment and the meanings of sexuality* Carabine argues that there are possibilities for renegotiating the meanings of sexuality. She, too, is critical of assumptions that sexuality is primarily a biological matter. Such essentialist assumptions can have oppressive consequences. One implication of her comments is that there is clearly more to empowerment in relation to sexual identity than making superficial changes.
- *Identity and difference* A person's identity is not fixed. It is something that is changeable in relation to multiple differences. In view of this, there can be no single way of taking empowerment forward. Different people will seek empowerment in different ways because of these differences in identity.

- *Resistance and empowerment* She argues that the relationship between resistant power relationships and empowerment is a complex one. She points out that empowerment can involve resistance but does not have to, for example, empowerment can be achieved by embracing existing power relations as equal rights approaches tend to do. Her basic point is that the notion of resistance is generally underdeveloped and in need of further attention.

Carabine's comments illustrate the complexity of the matters we are seeking to address. There is clearly, therefore, a great need to develop our understanding in more depth. One positive aspect of this situation is that there is now a growing literature on matters relating to sexuality and sexual identity (see Part Four). It is to be hoped that, by developing our knowledge of these complex issues, we can be in a stronger position to challenge the disempowering effects of discrimination based on an unfair discourse of the supposed naturalness of heterosexuality.

## Conclusion

The other areas of discrimination we have explored in Part Three have shown themselves to involve complex sets of issues. Sexual identity is no exception. Promoting empowering forms of practice needs to be a broad-based undertaking to ensure that important parts of people's lives, such as sexual identity, are not neglected. Once again, there are no easy answers, but it is to be hoped that the discussions in this chapter have helped to raise awareness and to lay down a foundation for further learning.

## Points to ponder

➤ In what ways might sexual identity be relevant to your line of work?
➤ How might heterosexism manifest itself?
➤ What steps towards tackling heterosexism could you and your colleagues take?

# Chapter 13
# Religion

Like sexuality, religion is something that can be both a deeply personal matter and a reflection of wider society. It is also something that can be a source of considerable discrimination and therefore a significant obstacle to empowerment. Attempts to develop empowering forms of practice would therefore do well to take account of the significance of religion and how religion-related discrimination can be a major problem.

## Religious discrimination

The significance of religion in modern society is clearly of major proportions. Although there is reason to believe that religious influences are declining in some respects, there is also overwhelming evidence that religion remains a major feature of the lives of a significant proportion of the world's population. Within the UK there are particular issues. For example, in Northern Ireland there has been a long history of sectarianism (a form of discrimination that manifests itself in other parts of the UK as well, albeit to a lesser extent). There have also been more recent tensions as a result of terrorism, with some people narrow-mindedly equating people of Muslim faith with terrorism. Pilkington (2003) describes it in the following terms:

> the representation of the events on 11 September 2001 as the responsibility of fundamentalist Muslims has generated a racist backlash directed at Muslims in most Western countries, including Britain.
> In Britain the government and the media have been at pains to point out that the enemy is terrorism and not Islam, and Muslim organisations have condemned the attacks as un-Islamic. Despite this, British Muslims have been subject to increasing racist harassment and have felt intimidated about voicing their opposition to the bombing campaign in Afghanistan for fear of reprisals. Since 11 September 'to be a Muslim is to be under suspicion, under threat and, given the huge increase in racial violence, under attack' (Younge 2001). (pp. 276–7)

People can be discriminated against on the grounds of their religious faith or a particular sect within their religious faith, hence the term sectarianism. Discrimination on the grounds of religion or sect is often part and parcel of racism, but it can also be a significant issue in its own right. That is, discrimination can arise between groups who are not generally seen as reflecting different racial groups, but who are, none the less, seen as antagonists in terms of their religious commitments.

## Responding to religious needs

Religious discrimination can arise as a result of bigotry and religious hatred. However, it can also arise, like institutional racism and indeed disablism, from a failure to address non-mainstream needs. That is, people of a particular faith can suffer a detriment because services are not geared towards meeting their needs.

It is not possible for human services practitioners and managers to be conversant with all aspects of all religions (or even the main ones), but we can (and should):

- *have at least a rudimentary understanding of the basics* A good basic knowledge of the main religions can be a useful starting point and can help to sensitise us to key differences and issues.
- *know how to find out further information as and when required (and be prepared to do so)* Foundational and more advanced-level information is readily available in various books and, of course, from the Internet.
- *be prepared to use our communication and rapport-building skills to learn more* In this way we can make sure that our actions are appropriate in relation to the religion and culture of the people we are trying to help.

In relation to the last of these three points, we should be wary of making the mistake of assuming that religion is something that is experienced by members of a particular faith in a standard or uniform way. How religion is lived and experienced by the individuals concerned will vary enormously. For example, how one person understands and lives their Catholicism may be very different indeed from how another person understands and lives their Catholicism. A blanket approach to religion is not appropriate, as that is far too simplistic an understanding of a very complex aspect of human reality.

---

### Practice Focus 13.1

Lisa was aware of the importance of taking people's religious beliefs and needs into account, but it was only when she started to appreciate the sheer diversity of religious groups in her area that she realised how huge a task this was. She began by devoting a lot of time to learning as much as she could but when she came to realise that what it said in the books and so on about particular religions did not necessarily match the way specific people actually lived their faith, she felt it was a hopeless task. However, she recognised how important it was to address the religious and spiritual dimensions of people's lives, and so she set herself the much more manageable target of learning the basics and building on these over time, while all the time staying open to understanding how particular individuals and families lived their faith.

---

## Promoting empowerment

A helpful step forward in the UK was the implementation in 2003 of the regulations against religious discrimination. This was a significant step forward in terms of giving a clear message that discrimination on the grounds of religion was not acceptable. However, as we have learned in relation to sex and race discrimination (and, more recently, disability discrimination), the law is a fairly blunt instrument and one that is certainly not enough on its own. Some degree of legal backing on these matters is none the less a welcome development.

However, just as an emphasis on diversity as an asset to be celebrated has featured in the equalities field in recent years, we can see this as a positive way of responding to religious issues. Valuing diversity means recognising the benefits of having people from different backgrounds, with different perspectives and different contributions to make. This may lead to conflicts and tensions at times, but the overall picture that diversity paints is one of *enrichment* as a result of the breadth of perspective and vision it brings.

We encounter enormous complications when we address religious issues. If we are not to be disempowering, we need to be:

- *prepared to engage with these complexities and not gloss over them* As with issues of race and culture in particular and equality more broadly, religious matters can be very sensitive. It is therefore understandable – but not necessarily acceptable – that many people steer clear of engaging with these complex and intricate issues.
- *prepared to listen and learn* It is vital that we are open to learning. It is very easy to alienate people (and thus fail to support them in their efforts to empower themselves) by not being sufficiently aware of what matters to members of a particular faith.
- *open minded* Prejudices about particular religions commonly feature in discourses that are quite influential at the cultural level. We therefore have to 'unlearn' any stereotypical or biased assumptions that we have been exposed to as part of our upbringing.

The challenge of empowerment in relation to religion is a significant one. What has not helped is that matters of religion and spirituality have tended to be neglected in professional education in the human services (Moss, 2005), and it is only relatively recently that we have begun to take seriously the nature and extent of the issues we need to address. However, what is clear is that it is not possible to get away with simply seeing religion as a dimension of race or ethnicity and therefore not taking it seriously as a set of issues in its own right.

Making empowerment a reality in relation to religion is not a matter of following simple instructions or adopting formula solutions. Rather, it is a matter of wrestling with the complexities, supporting one another in broadening and deepening our understanding over time. It is also, of course, a matter of continuing to emphasise the strengths of working in partnership and supporting the user involvement movement.

## Conclusion

For very many people being a member of a faith community is a tremendous source of 'power with' and an excellent basis for developing 'power from within'. However, as a result of the discrimination associated with religion, it is also possible for members of a religion to face considerable disempowerment. The challenge we face is to make sure, as far as we reasonably can, that the positives are to the fore, with the processes that lead to disempowerment kept to a minimum and challenged wherever possible.

## Points to ponder

➤ How might your own beliefs about religion and spirituality affect your work?
➤ Do you know how to find out about any particular religious faith or sect you may encounter?
➤ How can you play a part in tackling religious discrimination?

# Chapter 14
# Class

Class can be defined as a 'socio-economic group'. In other words, the notion of class is a way of dividing people up in terms of their social position and economic ranking (that is, relating to their income and access to financial resources – savings, stocks, shares, property and other such assets). Of course, limited access to financial resources can be very disempowering in itself, but it can also lead to wider problems in terms of inequalities in relation to such matters as education, health and criminal justice as well as various others. These can reinforce one another and, indeed, interact with other forms of discrimination such as sexism, racism and ageism.

## The significance of poverty

The impact of poverty can be quite devastating. This is because its effects can be both broad and deep:

- *Breadth* Poverty can have a detrimental effect on a wide variety of aspects of people's lives, including psychological factors (self-esteem, for example), social issues (relationships and social standing) and health (both physical and mental).
- *Depth* The impact of poverty can be very intense and profound.

The following comments from Novak (1996) illustrate this well:

> Poverty is a problem the effects of which are felt in a myriad of different ways: in hunger and early death, in poor health, despair and depression, in the corrosion of people's well-being and social relationships, and in frustration and anger. As such, poverty lies at the root of, and contributes significantly to, many other social problems, to growing levels of social tension, to racism and other forms of violence. It is a problem of immense proportions, both in the numbers whose lives are disfigured by it and in the scale and nature of change required to eradicate it. It is about power and control over resources, and the solution to the problem – fundamental and long-term though it may be – can only be to return that power to those who have been dispossessed of it. (p. 85)

Novak also makes the important point that empowerment for poor people is significantly different from what other groups of people are trying to achieve in their efforts in this direction. This difference lies in the fact that other disadvantaged groups working towards empowerment base much of their work on pride, valuing what has historically and ideologically been devalued – for example, alternative forms of sexuality, disabled lifestyles and so on. However, there is no pride to be taken in poverty.

Empowerment is therefore about enabling people to get out of poverty and work towards eradicating it. There can be some degree of pride in terms of the resilience that is necessary to cope with poverty, and there is certainly much in the way of strengths to be found in those communities where poverty is a significant issue. However, this does not alter the fact that Novak is correct in identifying class-related empowerment as having a different basis from other forms of emancipatory projects.

---

### Practice Focus 14.1

George had previously been involved in a project relating to promoting positive race relations. He was therefore quite well tuned in to issues about empowerment and the need to tackle oppressive discourses and structures that held people back and prevented them from fulfilling their potential. In particular, he was committed to what he called 'accentuating the positives' – by which he meant helping people find pride in their culture and ethnic identity. However, when he moved to a new post that had been created as part of an anti-poverty strategy, he initially found it difficulty to adapt his previous experience. At first, he wondered how he could help people to take pride in poverty and began to fear that he had made a mistake in moving to this post. However, before too long, he got to know many of the people in the communities he was working with and started to recognise the great strengths there. He came to acknowledge that, for example, doing a good job of bringing up children on benefits in a deprived area was a highly skilled and demanding task and something to be enormously proud of. He began to think about how he could build on this in his future work.

---

## Tackling poverty

There have been long debates about whether human services can make a meaningful contribution towards tackling poverty. While poverty is clearly a political matter at a macro level and thus beyond the reach of human services practitioners in many ways, we can none the less make a significant contribution in the following ways:

- Take whatever steps we reasonably can at a micro level to tackle poverty. This can include, for example, welfare rights advocacy where appropriate. It is important not to be defeatist about this and assume there is little or nothing that can be done. This level of intervention will not make a major difference to poverty as a social problem overall, but it can make a very significant positive contribution to the life and well-being of very many people.

- Take account of the impact of poverty on the problems we are addressing (in relation to health care, social care, community justice, and so on). Commonly poverty will exacerbate other problems – often in quite significant ways. We should not underestimate how much of a factor poverty can be in problems that initially seem unconnected with it.
- Not be judgemental by relying on class-based stereotypes. For example, a commonly encountered stereotype is that people who live in poverty are of low intelligence and have little to offer. Consider the following comment from Galloway (2002):

  'The worst thing about living in poverty is the way it gives others permission to treat you – as if you don't matter.' Statement by group of low income parents to the APPGP [All Party Parliamentary Group on Poverty]. (p. 13, cited in Lister, 2004, p. 99)

- Contributing to wider campaigns for social inclusion – personally and professionally – wherever possible. Individually and collectively there is much that can be done to bring about change – consider, for example, the work done under the 'Make Poverty History' banner in 2005.

## Multiple oppressions

Being poor and/or being stigmatised for being a member of a particular class group can seriously damage a person's health, well-being, life chances, and so on. We therefore have to make sure that we do not neglect such matters in taking forward our commitment to empowering forms of practice. This is particularly important when we can recognise that class-related issues are also significant in relation to other forms of discrimination. Consider the following examples:

- *sexism* Many people (especially women) experience what is known as 'secondary poverty'. This refers to households where the overall level of income is sufficient for the family's needs, but one member of the family is taking more than their fair share of it (for drinking or gambling, for example).
- *racism* Due to decades of racial discrimination, people from ethnic minorities are over-represented in the lower income levels and are therefore more likely to experience poverty and deprivation.
- *ageism* We can note that older people are more prone to poverty than other age groups within the range of the life course. This is partly connected with pensions policies over the years.
- *disablism* Disabled people are more likely to be unemployed than non-disabled people, and so poverty and disability can be closely intertwined.
- *heterosexism* People in the lower levels of the income range are likely to have fewer resources for escaping the stigma still associated with same-sex relationships. That is, wealth can buy a certain degree of protection from the negative effects of heterosexism.

- *religious discrimination* Poverty can exacerbate religious and sectarian tensions (as indeed it can for other forms of tension too).

As I have argued previously (Thompson, 2006c), it is important to recognise that different forms of discrimination interconnect and reinforce each other. They need to be seen as dimensions of people's experience, and not as isolated factors in their own right.

This tendency for class issues to exacerbate other forms of discrimination adds further urgency to the need to tackle issues of poverty and class-based discrimination in whatever ways we reasonably can.

## Conclusion

Class and poverty issues have been left to the last chapter not because they are less important than what has preceded them, but rather to emphasise that class is a factor that relates to each of the areas covered (and indeed to others that we have not had space to cover, such as language-related discrimination). In a sense, it is a bedrock of all the other areas of discrimination and oppression we have examined. Two clear implications of this are:

- efforts to promote empowering forms of practice in relation to the various forms of discrimination must also address the class and poverty dimension; and
- empowerment in relation to class and poverty is a worthwhile goal to be pursued in its own right.

## Points to ponder

➤ How does class feature as a dimension of your line of work?
➤ What significance does poverty have for the people you seek to help?
➤ How can you help to promote empowerment as part of tackling poverty?

# Part Four: Guide to Further Learning

## Introduction

The point was made at the beginning of the book that this is an introductory text and not one that aims to be comprehensive or exhaustive. A more realistic aim for a book such as this is to provide a basic level of understanding and lay the foundations for developing your knowledge and skills over time. Part Four is therefore very important in so far as it provides guidance on further reading and access to internet resources. You are strongly encouraged to read widely on the subjects of power and empowerment for, as I have emphasised earlier, these are not only complex issues, but also very important ones.

It is to be hoped that, having read Parts One to Three, you will have developed a clearer picture of what is involved in power and empowerment and why they are so important. However, it would be a major mistake to allow this to instil a degree of complacency and leave you feeling that you know all that you need to know. Please do, therefore, take the time and trouble to make full use of Part Four as a gateway to further learning.

### Further reading

There is a vast literature on the subjects of power and empowerment. What appears below is therefore only a selection of what is available and is certainly not a comprehensive bibliography.

#### *Power*

For a philosophical approach to power, see Morriss (2002) and Russell (2004).

A very good account of sociological perspectives is to be found in Westwood (2002). Lukes (2005) is a revised and expanded edition of a classic text.

The poststructuralist approach associated with Foucault is discussed in Faubion (2002) and Tew (2002).

For discussions of power relating to human services, see Tew (2002), Thompson (2003a), Thompson (2006c) and Hugman (1991).

The power of language is discussed in Thompson (2003b). For a specifically feminist analysis, see Cameron (1998) and/or Sunderland (2004).

For an interesting discussion of media power, see McCullagh (2002). Mitchell and Schoeffel (2003) and Herman and Chomsky (1994) are also interesting and thought-provoking sources relating to the work of Noam Chomsky.

For a discussion of power that is totally devoid of ethics, integrity and compassion, see Greene (2000).

Structuration theory is discussed in Stones (2005) and Thompson (2003a).

### Empowerment

Adams (2003) is a good general introduction, and Braye and Preston-Shoot (1995) also has much to commend it. Humphries (1996) offers an excellent critical perspective.

Empowerment in relation to older people is discussed in Thursz *et al.* (1995), Bounds and Hepburn (1996) and Sue Thompson (2005). See also Thompson and Thompson (2001).

Ramcharan, P., Roberts, G., Grant, G. and Borland, J. (1996) *Empowerment in Everyday Life: Learning Disability,* London, Jessica Kingsley.

Swain *et al.* (2004) is a good starting point for exploring empowerment in relation to disability. Issues relating specifically to *learning* disabilities are explored in Ramcharan *et al.* (1996).

Task-centred practice and groupwork are both important methods of intervention when it comes to promoting empowerment – see Marsh and Doel (2005) and Doel (2006) respectively.

Mental health issues are covered in Barnes and Bowl (2001) and Linhorst (2006).

### Employee empowerment and staff care

Empowerment in relation to organisation and management issues has a large literature. See, for example, Blanchard *et al.* (2001a, 2001b).

### Partnership

Carnwell and Buchanan (2004) and Harrison *et al.* (2003) both offer considerable food for thought on this subject.

Leathard (2003), Sullivan and Skelcher (2002) and Weinstein *et al.* (2003) are also useful sources.

### User involvement

The Social Care Institute for Excellence has produced a helpful report: (SCIE, 2004). Other useful texts include: Kemshall and Littlechild (2000), Minhas (2005) and Shaping Our Lives National User Network (2003).

## *Professionalism*

Payne (2006) provides an interesting analysis of professionalism in social work and social care, as does Davies (2000). Thompson (2002) addresses professionalism in child care.

## *Discrimination and oppression*

Thompson (2006c) is an introductory text on discrimination and oppression in social work (although widely used by staff and students from other professional groups), while Thompson (2003a) is a more in-depth examination of the subject with a focus much broader than social work.

Kallen (2004) is a useful text on inequality which focuses specifically on human rights aspects. Baker *et al.* (2004) is also a useful source on equality issues.

Difference and discrimination in psychotherapy and counselling are discussed in Marshall (2004). Equality and diversity issues in health care are explored in Baxter (2001).

Morland and Willox (2005) is a thought-provoking set of readings about sexuality.

The diversity approach is presented in Kandola and Fullerton (1998). Anderson (2003) is a short but helpful text.

## Training resources

Thompson (2005b) addresses equality and diversity issues across a wide variety of work and professional settings, while Castle and Moss (2005) focus specifically on disability equality issues (www.learningcurvepublishing.co.uk).

Kandola, R. and Fullerton, J. (1998) *Tools for Managing Diversity*, London, Chartered Institute of Personnel and Development.

Dadzie, S. (2000) *Toolkit for Tackling Racism in Schools*, Stoke on Trent, Trentham Books.

## Organisations and websites

### *Empowerment*

National Empowerment Center http://www.power2u.org/

A US-based mental health site focusing on recovery.

Protecting Women http://protectingwomen.com/

A US-based site concerned with 'Empowering Women Through Knowledge'. It focuses on protection from violence through self-defence.

Empowerment Project

US-based site providing support and advocacy for gay, lesbian, bisexual, transgender and questioning youth and young adults.
http://www.chd-prevention.org/emp_index.htm

Empowerment Resources

Another US-based site, this time with an emphasis on green issues.
http://www.empowermentresources.com/

Youth Empowerment Scheme

Northern Ireland site aiming to support social inclusion of young people.
http://www.youthempowermentscheme.org/

Q Web – Women's Empowerment Base

A Swedish site geared towards gender equality and health issues.
http://www.qweb.kvinnoforum.se/

## *User involvement*

Age Concern www.ace.org.uk
Astral House
1268 London Road
London SW16 4ER

British Institute of Learning Disabilities www.bild.org.uk
Campion House
Green Street
Kidderminster
Worcestershire DY10 1JL
Tel: 01562 723010

MIND www.mind.org.uk
National Association for Mental Health
Infoline: 0845 7660163

## *Equality and diversity organisations*

Age Positive www.agepositive.gov.uk
Department for Work and Pensions
Room W8d
Moorfoot
Sheffield S1 4PQ

Commission for Racial Equality www.cre.gov.uk
Elliot House
10–12 Allington Street
London SW1E 5EH
Tel: 020 7828 7022

DIALOG www.lg-employers.gov.uk/diversity

Disability Rights Commission www.drc-gb.org
Freepost MID02164
Stratford upon Avon CV37 9BR
Tel: 08457 622 633
Textphone: 08457 622 644

Equality Direct www.equalitydirect.org.uk
Tel: 0845 600 3444

Equal Opportunities Commission www.eoc.org.uk
Overseas House
Quay St
Manchester M3 3HN
Tel: 0161 833 9244

Lesbian and Gay Foundation www.lgf.org.uk

National Bullying Advice Line www.successunlimited.co.uk

Stonewall www.stonewall.org.uk

# Conclusion

A theme throughout this book has been the legacy of oversimplification that we have encountered in so many different areas of the study and practice of empowerment. Morriss (2002) offers apt comment when he argues that:

> But, despite the term 'empowerment' being currently fashionable, very little of the literature that I have read has bothered to include any discussion of exactly *what* the power is that empowerment should produce. It does seem clear that at issue here is the ability (of hitherto marginalized groups) to achieve, obtain or do things. As Allen put it, 'in the empowerment theoretical view, power is a capacity or creative ability that individuals have *to do* something. ... This conception sees power as the capacity or ability to pursue certain life projects.' This must presumably involve the realization of some of the individuals' latent powers; it seems that those who are satisfactorily empowered now have the power to do a range of (important) things, and that that is seen as a good thing. ... However, I think that the demand for empowerment would be more persuasive if it included a more rigorous examination of the sort of power that was thought desirable . . . (p. xxvi)

We therefore clearly have to be very wary of this danger of oversimplification. This means that we have to appreciate the complexities and subtleties of both power and empowerment and be prepared to engage our analytical skills and critical faculties in making sense of these issues and trying to put them into practice.

Power and empowerment issues are closely related to matters of inequality, discrimination and oppression. A key theme, therefore, must be that of struggle. Any approach that offers clear-cut, simple answers is clearly a dangerous misrepresentation of the reality. Power and empowerment are topics that need to be approached with caution, as they can lead to considerable difficulties if we do not take account of how complex they are both in their own right and in terms of the interrelationship between the two of them. Simply trying to understand them is an undertaking of significant proportions because of the complexities of the theory base, but when we combine that with trying to put these into practice as well, we are clearly dealing with a situation of immense complexity and challenge. Partly what makes it so complex is that empowerment has its roots in the wider world of politics. We therefore need to reiterate the point made earlier in the book that we should not try to understand empowerment without locating it within this broader picture of political struggles to achieve equality and social justice in a very unequal world.

Adams (2003) makes the point that empowerment can be seen as 'transform- ational'. I understand this to mean that it presents a major challenge to how services are organised, managed, directed and delivered. It will certainly not be enough to make minor adjustments to how traditional approaches to human services practice and management are undertaken. The real challenge of empowerment as part of a broader tableau of tackling inequality and promoting social justice is to retain those aspects of established practices that are positive, life-enhancing and genuinely contributing to health and well-being of the people we are trying to help and to change those aspects that are paternalistic and unsympathetic to the demands of empowerment.

We should not forget the significance of humility in all this. We should not overstate the potential for empowerment, because there are clearly major political, organisational and historical obstacles to taking empowerment forward in the ways that we would like to. However, we should not underestimate the potential for empowerment either. Defeatism does not help. It is not only problematic in its own right, it can block empowerment or even actively disempower those people that we are attempting to support. Again, it is a matter of realism, being neither overoptimistic nor unduly defeatist.

Power and empowerment are subjects that have been prone to a great deal of rhetoric, often without the depth of analysis needed to accompany such important topics. Sadly, this in itself can be seen as a misuse of power. Some people who have been in positions to help take forward a project of empower- ment have actually proven to be counterproductive by alienating people who would otherwise perhaps have been prepared to show a commitment while also supporting (unwittingly perhaps) forms of practice that are so crude and simplistic that they do not do justice to the challenge that we face. What is needed, then, is an authentic approach to empowerment, one that goes beyond empty rhetoric and devotes the time, effort and energy needed to make sense of the complexities and, moreover, the major challenges of putting such complex ideas into practice.

# References

Abers, R. (1998) 'From Clientelism to Cooperation: Local Government, Participatory Policy, and Civil Organizing in Porto Alegre, Brazil', *Politics and Society*, 26 pp. 511–37.

Adams, R. (2003) *Social Work and Empowerment*, 3rd edn, Basingstoke, Palgrave Macmillan.

Allen, A. (1999) *The Power of Feminist Theory: Domination, Resistance, Solidarity*, Boulder, Col., Westview Press.

Afshar, H. (ed.) (1998) *Women and Empowerment: Illustrations from the Third World*, Basingstoke, Macmillan – now Palgrave Macmillan.

Anderson, T. with Metcalf, H. (2003) *Diversity: Stacking Up the Evidence*, London, The Chartered Institute of Personnel and Development.

Bachrach, P. and Baratz, M.S. (1970) *Power and Poverty: Theory and Practice*, Oxford and New York, Oxford University Press.

Baiochhi, G. (2003) 'Participation, Activism and Politics: The Porto Alegre Experiment', in Fung and Wright (2003).

Baker, J., Lynch, K., Cantillon, S. and Walsh, J. (2004) *Equality: From Theory to Action*, Basingstoke, Palgrave Macmillan.

Barnes, M. and Bowl, R. (2001) *Taking Over the Asylum: Empowerment and Mental Health*, Basingstoke, Palgrave Macmillan.

Baxter, E. (ed.) (2001) *Managing Diversity and Inequality in Health Care*, London, Bailliere-Tindall.

Beauvoir, S. de (1972) *The Second Sex*, Harmondsworth, Penguin.

Becker, H.S. (1967) 'Whose Side Are We On?' *Social Problems*, 14(3).

Blanchard, K., Carlos, J.P. and Randolph, A. (2001a) *The 3 Keys to Empowerment: Release the Power Within People for Astonishing Results*, San Francisco, CA, Berrett-Koehler.

Blanchard, K., Carlos, J.P. and Randolph, A. (2001b) *Empowerment Takes More Than a Minute*, San Francisco, CA, Berrett-Koehler.

Bounds, J. and Hepburn, H. (1996) *Empowerment and Older People*, Birmingham, Pepar.

Brandon, D. (2000) *Tao of Survival: Spirituality in Social Care and Counselling*, Birmingham, Venture Press.

Braye, S. and Preston-Shoot, M. (1995) *Empowering Practice in Social Care*, Buckingham, Open University Press.

Bryson, B. (1990) *The Lost Continent: Travels in Small Town America*, London, Abacus.

Cameron, D. (ed.) (1998) *The Feminist Critique of Language: A Reader*, London, Routledge.

Carabine, J. (1996) 'Empowering Sexualities', in Humphries (1996).

Carabine, J. (2004a) 'Sexualities, Personal Lives and Social Policy', in Carabine (2004b).

Carabine, J. (ed.) (2004b) *Sexualities, Personal Lives and Social Policy*, Bristol, The Policy Press.

Carnwell, R. and Buchanan, J. (eds) (2004) *Effective Practice in Health and Social Care*, Maidenhead, Open University Press.

Cassell, P. (1993) *The Giddens Reader*, Basingstoke, Macmillan – now Palgrave Macmillan.

Castle, R. and Moss, B. (2005) *Understanding Disability: A Training Resource Pack*, Wrexham, Learning Curve Publishing.

Craib, I. (1976) *Existentialism and Sociology*, Cambridge, Cambridge University Press.

Croft, S. and Beresford, P. (2000) 'Empowerment', in Davies (2000).

Cumming, E. and Henry, W.E. (1961) *Growing Old*, New York, Basic Books.

Dahl, R.A. (1957) 'A Rejoinder', *American Political Science Review* 55, pp. 1053–61.

Dadzie, S. (2000) *Toolkit for Tackling Racism in Schools*, Stoke on Trent, Trentham Books.

Davies, C. (2003) 'Workers, Professions and Identity', in Henderson and Atkinson (2003).

Davies, M. (ed.) (2000) *The Blackwell Encyclopaedia of Social Work*, Oxford, Blackwell.

Deegan, P.E. (1997) 'Recovery and Empowerment for People with Psychiatric Disabilities', *Social Work in Health Care*, 25(3).

Denzin, N. and Lincoln, Y. (eds) (1994) *Handbook of Qualitative Research*, Ann Arbor, University of Michigan Press.

Department of Health (1998) *Independent Inquiry into Inequalities and Health Report* (Chaired by Sir Donald Acheson), Norwich, The Stationery Office.

Doel, M. (2006) *Using Groupwork*, London, Routlege.

Donelan, B. (1995) 'Empowerment as Illustrated by a Bear, Napoleon and Others', in Thursz *et al.* (1995).

Dowding, K. (1996) *Power*, Buckingham, Open University Press.

Eastman, M. (1995) 'User First – Implications for Management', in Jack (1995).

Ellis, K. (1992) *Squaring the Circle: User and Carer Participation in Needs Assessment*, York, Joseph Rowntree Foundation.

Fanon, F. (1967) *Black Skin, White Masks*, New York, Grove Press.

Faubion, J.D. (ed.) (2002) *Power: Essential Works of Foucault 1954–1984, Vol 3*, London, Penguin.

Fine, M. (1994) 'Working the Hyphens: Reinventing Self and Other in Qualitative Research', in Denzin and Lincoln (1994).

Fook, J. (2002) *Social Work: Critical Theory and Practice*, London, Sage.

Foucault, M. (1977) *Discipline and Punish: The Birth of the Prison*, London, Tavistock.

Foucault, M. (1978) *The History of Sexuality, Vol 1: An Introduction* (trans Hurley, R.), New York, Pantheon.

Frazer, N. and Gordon, L. (1994) 'Civil Citizenship Against Social Citizenship? On the Ideology of Contract-versus-charity', in van Steenbergen (1994).

Fung, A. (2003) 'Deliberative Democracy, Chicago Style: Grassroots Governance in Policing and Public Education', in Fung and Wright (2003).

Fung, A. and Wright, E.O. (eds) (2003) *Deepening Democracy: Institutional Innovations in Empowered Participatory Governance*, London, Verso.

Galloway, K. (2002) *A Scotland Where Everyone Matters*, Manchester, Church Action on Poverty.

Giddens, A. (1994) *Beyond Left and Right*, Cambridge, Polity Press.

Gomm, R. (1993) 'Issues of Power in Health and Welfare', in Walmsley *et al.* (1993).

Gould, N. and Baldwin, M. (eds) (2004) *Social Work, Critical Reflection and the Learning Organization*, Aldershot, Ashgate.

Greene, R. (2000) *The 48 Laws of Power*, London, Profile Books.

Harrison, R., Mann, G., Murphy, M., Taylor, A. and Thompson, N. (2003) *Partnership Made Painless*, Lyme Regis, Russell House Publishing.

Healy, K. (2000) *Social Work Practices: Contemporary Perspectives on Change*, London, Sage.

Henderson, J. and Atkinson, D. (eds) (2003) *Managing Care in Context*, London, Routledge.

Herman, E.S. and Chomsky, N. (1994) *Manufacturing Consent: The Political Economy of the Mass Media*, London, Vintage.

Hughes, B. (2004) 'Disability and the Body', in Swain *et al.* (2004).

Hugman, R. (1991) *Power in Caring Professions*, Basingstoke, Macmillan Education.

Humphries, B. (ed.) (1996) *Critical Perspectives on Empowerment*, Birmingham, Venture Press.

Illich, I. (1976) *Limits to Medicine: The Expropriation of Health*, London, Marion Boyars.

Jack, R. (ed.) (1995) *Empowerment in Community Care*, London, Chapman and Hall.

Jones, C. (1996) 'Anti-intellectualism and the Peculiarities of British Social Work Education', in Parton (1996).

Jones, L.J. (1994) *The Social Context of Health and Health Work*, Basingstoke, Macmillan – now Palgrave Macmillan.

Kallen, E. (2004) *Social Inequality and Social Injustice*, Basingstoke, Palgrave Macmillan.

Kandola, R. and Fullerton, J. (1998) *Diversity in Action: Managing the Mosaic*, 2nd edn, London, Chartered Institute of Personnel and Development.

Kemshall, H. and Littlechild, R. (eds) (2000) *User Involvement and Participation in Social Care: Research Informing Practice*, London, Jessica Kingsley.

Langellier, K.M. and Peterson, E. E. (1993) Family Story Telling as a Strategy of Social Control, in Mumby, D.K. (ed.) *Narrative and Social Control: Critical Perspectives,* London: Sage.

Laurance, J. (2003) *Pure Madness: How Fear Drives the Mental Health System*, London, Routledge.

Leathard, A. (ed.) (2003) *Interprofessional Collaboration: From Policy to Practice in Health and Social Care*, Hove, Brunner-Routledge.

Lewis, G. (2004a) ' "Do Not Go Gently . . .": Terrains of Citizenship and Landscapes of the Personal', in Lewis (2004b).

Lewis, G. (ed.) (2004b) *Citizenship: Personal Lives and Social Policy*, Bristol, The Policy Press.

Linhorst, D.M. (2005) *Empowering People with Severe Mental Illness: A Practical Guide*, Oxford, Oxford University Press.

Lister, R. (2004) *Poverty*, Cambridge, Polity.

Lukes, S. (2005) *Power: A Radical View*, 2nd edn, Basingstoke, Palgrave Macmillan.

Marsh, P. and Doel, M. (2005) *The Task-Centred Book*, London, Routledge.

Marsh, P. and Fisher, M. (1992) *Good Intentions: Developing Partnership in Social Services*, York, Joseph Rowntree Foundation.

Marshall, S. (2004) *Difference and Discrimination in Psychotherapy and Counselling*, London, Sage.

Martin, T.L. and Doka, K.J. (2000) *Men Don't Cry . . . Women Do: Transcending Gender Stereotypes of Grief*, Philadelphia, PA, Brunner/Mazel.

McCullagh, C. (2002) *Media Power: A Sociological Introduction*, Basingstoke, Palgrave Macmillan.

McGregor, D. (1987) *The Human Side of Enterprise*, Harmondsworth, Penguin.

Minhas, A. (2005) 'Dependent upon Outside Help: Reflections from a Service User' in Carnwell and Buchanan (2005).

Mitchell, P.R. and Schoefel, E. (eds) (2003) *Understanding Power – Noam Chomsky*, London, Vintage.

Morland, I. and Willox, A. (eds) (2005) *Queer Theory*, Basingstoke, Palgrave Macmillan.

Morriss, P. (2002) *Power: A Philosophical Analysis*, 2nd edn, Manchester, University of Manchester Press.

Moss, B. (2005) *Religion and Spirituality*, Lyme Regis, Russell House Publishing.

Mullins, L.J. (1996) *Management and Organisational Behaviour,* London: Sage.

Novak, T. (1996) 'Empowerment and the Politics of Poverty', in Humphries (1996).

Nusberg, C. (1995) 'Preface', in Thursz *et al.* (1995).

Oliver, M. (1990) *The Politics of Disablement.* Basingstoke, Palgrave Macmillan.

Ouchi, W.G. (1981) *Theory Z: How American Business Can Meet the Japanese Challenge*, Boston, MA, Addison-Wesley.

Parton, N. (ed.) (1996) *Social Theory, Social Change and Social Work*, London, Routledge.

Parton, N. and O'Byrne, P. (2000) *Constructive Social Work: Towards a New Practice*, Basingstoke, Macmillan – now Palgrave Macmillan.

Patton, P. (ed.) (1993) *Nietzsche, Feminism and Political Theory*, St Leonard's, NSW, Allen and Unwin.

Payne, M. (2006) *What is Professional Social Work?*, 2nd edn, Bristol, The Policy Press.

Pilkington, A. (2003) *Racial Disadvantage and Ethnic Diversity in Britain*, Basingstoke, Palgrave Macmillan.

Powell, F. (2001) *The Politics of Social Work*, London, Sage.

Rowlands, J. (1998) 'A Word of the Times, but What Does it Mean? Empowerment in the Discourse and Practice of Development', in Afshar (1998).

Russell, B. (2004) *Power: A New Social Analysis*, London, Routledge (originally published 1938).

Seligman, M.E.P. (1975) *Helplessness: On Depression, Development, and Death*, San Francisco, W.H. Freeman.

Servian, R. (1996) *Theorising Empowerment: Individual Power and Community Care*, Bristol, The Policy Press.

Shaping Our Lives National User Network (2003) *Shaping Our Lives: What People Think of The Social Care Services They Use*, York, Joseph Rowntree Foundation.

Shazer, S. de (1985) *Keys to Solutions in Brief Therapy*, New York, Norton.

Simon, B.L. (1990) 'Rethinking Empowerment', *Journal of Progressive Human Services*, 1 (1).

Smale, G., Tuson, G., with Biehal, N. and Marsh, P. (1993) *Empowerment, Assessment, Care Management and the Skilled Worker*, London, HMSO.

Social Care Institute for Excellence (2004) *Position Paper 3: Has Service User Involvement Made a Difference to Social Care Services?*, London, SCIE – downloadable from www.scie.org.uk.

Spender, D. (1980) *Man Made Language*, London, Routledge and Kegan Page.

Steenbergen, B. van (ed.) (1994) *The Condition of Citizenship*, London, Sage.

Stones, R. (2005) *Structuration Theory*, Basingstoke, Palgrave Macmillan.

Sullivan, S. and Skelcher, C. (2002) *Working Across Boundaries: Collaboration in Public Services*, Basingstoke, Palgrave Macmillan.

Sunderland, J. (2004) *Gendered Discourses,* Basingstoke, Palgrave Macmillan.

Swain, J., French, S., Barnes, C. and Thomas, C. (eds) (2004) *Disabling Barriers – Enabling Environments*, London, Sage.

Tapper, M. (1993) 'Ressentiment and Power: Some Reflections on Feminist Practices', in Patton (1993).

Tew, J. (2002) *Social Theory, Power and Practice*, Basingstoke, Palgrave Macmillan.

Thomas Isaac, T.M. and Heller, P. (2003) 'Democracy and Development: Decentralised Planning in Kerala', in Fung and Wright (2003).

Thompson, N. (2000) *Theory and Practice in Human Services*, 2nd edn, Buckingham, Open University Press.

Thompson, N. (2002) *Building the Future: Social Work with Children, Young People and their Families*, Lyme Regis, Russell House Publishing.

Thompson, N. (2003a) *Promoting Equality: Tackling Discrimination and Oppression*, 2nd edn, Basingstoke, Palgrave Macmillan.

Thompson, N. (2003b) *Communication and Language: A Handbook of Theory and Practice*, Basingstoke, Palgrave Macmillan.

Thompson, N. (2005a) *Understanding Social Work: Preparing for Practice*, 2nd edn, Basingstoke, Palgrave Macmillan.

Thompson, N. (2005b) *Promoting Equality, Valuing Diversity: A Training Resource Pack*, Wrexham, Learning Curve Publishing.

Thompson, N. (2006a) *People Problems*, Basingstoke, Palgrave Macmillan.

Thompson, N. (2006b) *Promoting Workplace Learning*, Bristol, The Policy Press.

Thompson, N. (2006c) *Anti-discriminatory Practice*, 4th edn, Basingstoke, Palgrave Macmillan.

Thompson, N. and Thompson, S. (2001) 'Empowering Older People: Beyond the Care Model', *Journal of Social Work* 1(1).

Thompson, N. and Thompson, S. (2005) *Community Care*, Lyme Regis, Russell House Publishing.

Thompson, S. (2005) *Age Discrimination*, Lyme Regis, Russell House Publishing.

Thompson, N., Murphy, M. and Stradling, S. (1994) *Dealing with Stress,* Basingstoke, Macmillan – now Palgrave Macmillan.

Thursz, D., Nusberg, C. and Prather, J. (eds) (1995) *Empowering Older People, An International Approach*, London, Cassell.

Turner, B.S. (1995) *Medical Power and Social Knowledge*, 2nd edn, London, Sage.

Walmsley, J., Reynolds, J., Shakespeare, P. and Woolfe, R. (eds) (1993) *Health and Welfare Practice: Reflecting on Roles and Relationships*, London, Sage.

Weinstein, J., Whittington, C. and Leiba, T. (eds) (2003) *Collaboration in Social Work Practice*, London, Jessica Kingsley.

Westwood, S. (2002) *Power and the Social*, London, Routledge.

Williams, S. with Seed, J. and Mwau, A. (1995) *The Oxfam Gender Training Manual*, Oxford, Oxfam.

Wirth, L. (2000) *Breaking Through the Glass Ceiling: Women in Management*, London, The Stationery Office.

Younge, G. (2001) 'The Right to be British', *The Guardian*, 12 November.

# Index